using BEAUTY and her BEAST

to introduce

the

Human

shadow

Kay
Newell
Plumb

using

BEAUTY

and her

BEAST

to introduce

the

Human

Shadow

Kay
Newell
Plumb

www.humanshadowtalk.com

Fairy tale text based on the 1757 version of *Beauty and the Beast*
Written by Jeanne-Marie Leprince de Beaumont
Translated by Marie Ponsot
Illustrated by Adrienne Segur

Illustrated by Bob Hobbs

Published in the United States by
WorldView Press
Portland, Oregon

ISBN: 978-0-9816708-0-5

Shelving categories:
1. Self-help—Psychology. 2.Current Events—USA

Printed in the United States of America

www.humanshadowtalk.com

" We are responsible for the effect of our
actions, and we are also responsible for
becoming as aware as we can of these effects."
- Rollo May

" The shadow is not necessarily
always an opponent.

In fact, it is exactly like any human being
with whom one has to get along.

Sometimes by giving in, sometimes
by resisting, sometimes by giving love -
whatever the situation requires.

The shadow becomes hostile only when it
is ignored or misunderstood. "

-Marie-Louise von Franz

Content

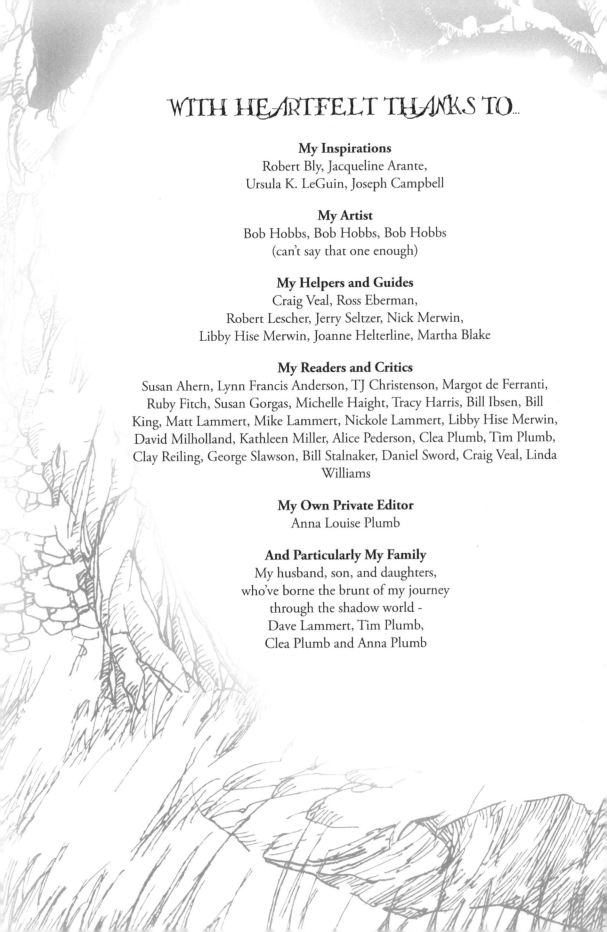

WITH HEARTFELT THANKS TO...

My Inspirations
Robert Bly, Jacqueline Arante,
Ursula K. LeGuin, Joseph Campbell

My Artist
Bob Hobbs, Bob Hobbs, Bob Hobbs
(can't say that one enough)

My Helpers and Guides
Craig Veal, Ross Eberman,
Robert Lescher, Jerry Seltzer, Nick Merwin,
Libby Hise Merwin, Joanne Helterline, Martha Blake

My Readers and Critics
Susan Ahern, Lynn Francis Anderson, TJ Christenson, Margot de Ferranti,
Ruby Fitch, Susan Gorgas, Michelle Haight, Tracy Harris, Bill Ibsen, Bill
King, Matt Lammert, Mike Lammert, Nickole Lammert, Libby Hise Merwin,
David Milholland, Kathleen Miller, Alice Pederson, Clea Plumb, Tim Plumb,
Clay Reiling, George Slawson, Bill Stalnaker, Daniel Sword, Craig Veal, Linda
Williams

My Own Private Editor
Anna Louise Plumb

And Particularly My Family
My husband, son, and daughters,
who've borne the brunt of my journey
through the shadow world -
Dave Lammert, Tim Plumb,
Clea Plumb and Anna Plumb

A Short Prologue containing

A Warning About Fairy Tales
&
An Explanation of Why This Book Does Not Get Right to the Point

Fairy tales aren't just simple—they're skeletal. In *Beauty and the Beast* we never learn Beauty's last name, her address, or her exact date of birth. That sort of fleshed-out fact decays after a few centuries. Only the bare bones live on in a classic fairy tale.[a]

Like many familiar things which seem harmless enough, fairy tales can be quite dangerous. They've become especially lethal in the last fifty years or so, with entertainment moguls selling them to a willing public as real life possibilities—*this could be you!*—when the truth is that any fairy tale will explode in your face if you try to reenact it here on the planet Earth. Your best—indeed, probably your *only*—defense against fairy tales is to keep in mind that the characters in fairy tales are not human beings.

Granted, this is not easy to remember. We all want to be as beautiful as the king's daughter or as brave as the handsome prince. Problem is, it just ain't humanly possible. The prince and the princess are "archetypes" airbrushed by centuries of repetition, not people. Although it is true that each character in a fairy tale represents a certain *aspect* of human nature, that aspect is only one bone in the psychic skeleton, not a complete human being.

These archetypes appeal to us because they're psychologically useful. Sometimes we need the fierceness of a witch, or the authority of a king, or the innocence of a child in the woods. But prolonged identification with any one archetype is not a good idea. At the very least you'll be sorely disappointed, and at the very worst you'll be dead—Marilyn Monroe, Kurt Cobain, Princess Di. A human being simply cannot live a fairy tale life. Consider yourself warned.

Beauty and the Beast belongs in a very old, very widespread category which folklorists call the "animal husband" story. Versions appear on prehistoric pottery, were specialties of the house when Zeus reigned from Olympus, and persist in many forms today. Why was *Dracula* such a ladies' man? What kept *The Mummy* alive for 4,000 years? Or how about *King Kong*? All he wanted was a little Fay Wray/Naomi Watts. We've watched Sigourney Weaver being impregnated by *Aliens* and adored by their offspring, and we've sympathized with the monster as he begged Dr. Frankenstein to make him a "F-f-f-rrrienndd…"

Once you start noticing the pattern, you'll see animal husband stories everywhere. Sci-fi, fantasy, horror—couldn't do without animal husbands. Which causes me to wonder: why does this type of story occur so often? Why do human beings have such a pronounced tendency to pair hideous monsters with comely maidens for entertainment purposes? And, can this tendency help me introduce the human shadow—an elusive psychological beastie; very difficult to catch in words—to the USA?

Turns out it can, but only with patience. If I head straight for the human shadow, off it goes. But if I don't try to pounce all over it with a scholarly introduction in the opening paragraphs, or force it out of hiding before it's ready to appear, the shadow stops running away from me and pricks up its ears. If I feign indifference, it creeps closer. I find that if I sit very still in the middle of a clearing, just retelling this old story with Bob's beautiful drawings and pretending to ignore it, the shadow eventually gets so curious about what I'm doing that it sidles right up to me and pushes its nose under my hand.

It's hard to look directly at the human shadow. The creature doesn't even exist all by itself. It only exists because people exist, and it can only be seen in the things that people do—their actions, ideas, hopes, fears, stories, dreams. Therefore this book will not even attempt to provide a definite sighting of the human shadow in the first few pages. This book will take a slower, more roundabout approach: it will shine a light on something else, something human—that familiar old story *Beauty and the Beast*—and then wait to see what comes up out of the darkness around it.

ONCE UPON A TIME

Or perhaps beneath a time...

Or maybe next to a time...

But certainly far beyond any time
you or I have ever been in...

... there was a rich merchant who had six children, three boys and three girls. All three daughters were pretty, but the youngest was beautiful. Indeed, as the years passed, she became so beautiful that everyone simply called her Beauty.

The two elder sisters were envious of Beauty, and missed no chance to make her miserable. These two were vain of their wealth and position. They liked to be seen with the richest people, going to the most exclusive parties. They enjoyed making fun of Beauty, who preferred to stay at home with their father, reading and playing music.

Where's Mama?

Something's missing here. What about dear old Mom? She's not even mentioned. We have no idea what happened to her. She's just—not there. We don't even get a cruel stepmother. Nothing. Since it usually takes some sort of mother to produce six children, it seems worth noting that there are no grown women in the beginning of this story.

Plus, the immature women we do get are out of whack. One daughter is modest, beautiful, and too attached to home, while the other daughters are jealous, spiteful, and too worldly. There's a real split here—Little Miss Virtue versus the Bad Grrlz—which tells us this story's problem lies in the feminine realm.

And that, easy as it was, is the first step in analyzing a classic fairy tale. Take a look at who's in the opening scene. In this case, since it's a family with scads of motherless children, we could even take a look at who *isn't* in the opening scene. Since each character in a classic fairy tale is an archetype— *"represents"* an instinctual element of human nature—then each character's presence or absence in a fairy tale *"stands for"* something.

It makes perfect sense, if you stop and think about it. Why do the same characters appear over and over in fairy tales all around the world? Because they're trying to say something to their cultures.

However, fairy tale characters have a little problem with delivery. They don't know how to speak in English—or Spanish or Greek or any other language. They only know how to speak in "symbol," the language of the collective unconscious, and the meaning of each symbol varies from person to person and from time to time. Even a universally recognized archetype like "mother" isn't cast in stone. She'll have a life of her own within you, and within your culture.

As an example of this insignificant sounding but actually rather important point, look at the symbol "serpent." On the ***collective imagery level***, the serpent was highly revered for thousands of years. Because he could shed his skin and be "reborn," because he could live in any element—on land, in water, in air—the

serpent symbolized rebirth and healing to the ancients. He wrapped himself around goddesses. He appeared on all the pottery and at all the important ceremonies. This reptile was just flat holy. But then the world began to change, and when the serpent slithered into a new mythological production being cast over in Eden, he wound up with the role of 'Satan's little helper.' It's the same reptile, it's the same symbol, but in our time he represents dread and evil.

On a ***personal imagery level*** for the symbol of serpent, I live in a cool damp climate where there aren't any poisonous snakes, so I think of snakes as harmless little garden helpers who eat slugs. If you live in a hot, dry climate where stepping on a snake could kill you, you might think of snakes as wicked, dangerous vermin.

That's how things change from place to place and from time to time. Any symbol, any archetype—like mother, like serpent—comes from, and is formed by, collective experiences of millions of human beings over thousands of years; but it has to be filtered through an individual to be understood, and filtered through the place and the time in which that individual lives.

So if we want to know what the symbol 'mother' means in this story, we might come up with Gaia the Great Earth Mother, or Eve the Temptress, or Mary the Virgin. We might think of the supportive home-style mother, always whipping up brownies or hot chocolate; or the corporate-style mother, always rushing off to work; or the destructive Medea-style mother, who murders her own children to spite her mate. Given enough time, any one of us could probably come up with a hundred meanings for 'mother,' spanning everything from coddling and culture to chaos and correction.

But—wait a minute. Where the hell are we going? There *is* no mother in this story. There's an *absence* of mother. There are no grown women at all, in fact. Which is strange, given all those offspring.

Where's Mama?

One day misfortune came to the merchant, and he lost all his riches. He was left with nothing but a small farm in the country. "We shall have to leave the city and live on the farm," he told his children. "But at least if we work hard we'll have plenty to eat, and for that we can be thankful."

On the farm, the merchant and his sons worked the fields. Beauty got up at dawn each day to clean the house and wash the clothes and cook the meals. She wasn't used to working, and it was hard at first. But she never complained, and soon she became capable and strong.

Her sisters, on the other hand, moped around moaning over their misfortune day after day, doing as little as possible.

Just to see Beauty working so willingly and so hard made them cross.

Too docile for your own damn good

Except for the shrew sisters, this looks pretty good, on the surface. Beauty seems like a nice girl, working hard to make the best of a bad situation, and her father and brothers sound heroic, getting to work right away on whatever needs to be done in a very manly fashion. It's a wonderful little scene, really. Kind of like a sitcom. *Father Knows Best* or *Full House* or *Family Matters.* Clearly identifiable good guys and bad guys—or girls.

The problem is, sitcoms do not happen in real life, and the surface isn't all we care about. Waters like these can have nasty undercurrents. Why should the older sisters get to shirk, complain, and be absolutely useless while Beauty takes on their work as well as her own? The story could use a good old scolding-type mama at this point, who'd nag those elder daughters back into line. But since there is no mother in this story, Beauty has to come up with her own solution. And since she's a one-dimensional figure, all sweetness and light, she comes up with a really simplistic solution. She acts like a martyr.

Does this sound vaguely familiar? Would you rather do someone else's work than confront them about not doing it themselves? Do you work more hours than you're paid to work? Do you do most of the picking up and putting away in your household?

Sometimes we act like martyrs because it seems easier than demanding that others do their fair share. Avoids conflict. And sometimes we act like martyrs to prove what fabulous people we are. Makes us feel righteous and hard-working. And sometimes we combine the two, since conflict avoidance and self-righteousness go together so well.

But only occasionally—very, very occasionally—is there any good reason whatsoever to act like a martyr, and the few people who do so under those circumstances become justifiably famous: Joan of Arc, Martin Luther King, Jr., Mahatma Gandhi. *{Terrorist martyrs? Forget it. We're not getting into anything quite that crazy in this book. And it's not something we do a lot of in the USA, anyway. Our mass murders are caused by alienation and self-absorption, not by misguided moral impulses.}*

Most of us are more like Beauty: we're just commonplace, garden variety, everyday, goody-goody, self-appointed martyrs. We wait on people who don't deserve it to keep from rocking the boat, we suffer in silence, and we waste precious hours of our own lives to do so, just as if we had hours to spare.

Doesn't seem like we've learned much since 1757, does it. Nowadays, aren't we supposed to know that Beauty is merely "enabling" her sisters to carry on with bad habits by not confronting them, that she's being the "co" to their "dependent" by acting this way? Nowadays, aren't we supposed to realize that not demanding justice merely contributes to injustice?

Theoretically. But somehow in actual practice we've gotten more complacent than ever. *We've Had 100 Years of Psychotherapy and the World's Getting Worse* as James Hillman and Michael Ventura say in one of their books.

We live in a democracy—one of those systems where people are supposed to govern themselves—but we tolerate blatantly criminal actions in high places; most of us earn wages that don't come close to keeping up with inflation or meeting the cost of living; we find ourselves with fewer social services, less funding for public education, and a bigger disparity between the top rung and the bottom rung every year; but still only about a third of us can get riled up enough to go out and vote on election day.

Nowadays, we apparently don't care who steps on us or how often they do so, as long as it doesn't interfere with our regularly scheduled entertainment.

Geez. Even back in Beauty's time, there was such a thing as being too docile for your own damn good.

After a year spent on the farm, good news came to the merchant. A ship he'd believed lost came into port, laden with cargo. As he made ready to go to the city to meet it, the elder sisters begged him to bring back clothes and jewels. They were wild with joy at the thought of being rich again.

"And what would you like?" the merchant asked Beauty as he turned to go.

"Perhaps you could bring me a rose, Father. We haven't any in our garden," answered Beauty.

She really couldn't think of a thing she wanted, but she knew better than to risk her sisters' wrath by saying so.

Know what you want, say what you mean

The rose is one of the oldest, most beloved, most frequently used icons for the feminine principle. On the symbolic level, Beauty just said, "Bring me back some Mama."

On the practical level, we're beginning to see why Beauty could use some animal husband as well as some Mama. She has a bad habit of being too good.

Her sisters are, of course, acting vilely, but couldn't Beauty have asked for something personal? A spool of thread? A book? New strings for her lute? No. Not Beauty. She denies—even to herself—that she wants anything at all—even the rose—*and it is this denial* that brings on the problems, not the Beast. Beauty's denial of her own needs, her refusal to even try to figure out what she really wants, brings a monster down on the whole family. In real life, this girl would be so passive-aggressive there'd be no living with her.

Selfishness is a basic human trait, an instinctual form of self-preservation, an archetypal way of acting, as Beauty's sisters demonstrate. Thus a human being cannot be totally unselfish. A human being can only recognize his or her innate capacity to be selfish, and try to keep a lid on it.

As Thomas Moore says in *Care of the Soul*, there's no curing certain things in ourselves.[c] All we can do is *care* for those things. But to take care of something, you have to—at the very least—be able to admit it exists. Pretending not to be selfish does not equal 'taking care of' your selfishness. Pretending not to be selfish equals *ignoring* your selfishness.

Besides, if we don't know what we want and how to go about getting it, why should anyone else? Should the rest of the world have to read our minds so we can get whatever we want without having to ask for anything? That can get real nasty in the real world. Not being able to just come out and say what you want—or what you mean, or what you feel—is the leading cause of resentment and divorce in the world.

But let's give Beauty the benefit of the doubt here. We just met her, and she seems *so* nice. Maybe she really doesn't want a single thing. Maybe she has completely conquered all desire, like a bodhisattva.

Then she should've said so, no matter what her sisters thought. Saying something she doesn't mean just to keep her sisters happy allows their bad attitudes to determine her actions.

Going along with something you don't agree with just to be polite is not civil—it's servile. And it's also downright dangerous, as we're about to find out.

In the city, the merchant was forced to use most of the money from the ship's cargo to pay old debts, and the rest to settle legal matters. As a result, after a great deal of trouble and anxiety, he started for home as poor as before.

Halfway there he entered a deep forest, where it began to snow so hard the merchant lost his way. Night fell, the wind raged, wolves howled. The merchant had no idea which way to turn.

Then he saw a gleam through the forest, and hurried toward it. At the end of a long, tree-lined drive, lights shone forth from every window of an enormous castle surrounded by beautifully tended gardens.

Gratefully the merchant galloped up to the elaborate bronze gates, which were standing wide open. But the courtyard was empty, and the stables, where the merchant tended to his tired horse, were also empty. Bewildered, the merchant went up to and through the intricately carved castle doors without seeing a soul.

Inside, he came upon a cheerful fire blazing in a fireplace and a table set for one near the hearth. Thinking, *The owners will surely pardon me for taking refuge here. They're bound to come soon,* he went up to the fire.

But he waited for hours, and no one came. Finally, being faint with hunger, the merchant sat down and ate. Then we walked through the adjoining rooms calling out, but still seeing no one, until at last he collapsed upon a fine bed in a magnificent bedroom and slept.

Falling into it

Darkness, debt, despair, loneliness, wild animals, stormy weather, gloomy forests—now we're cooking! These are all signs of 'falling action.' We're 'descending into the territory of the unconscious,' as a Jungian or a Freudian might say.

Un = under or opposite. Conscious = your thinking mind. *Un*conscious forces are the ones lying <u>under</u>neath your everyday, daylight, thinking mind. The forces you're generally not aware of, the ones that go on all by themselves.

Under? Around? Behind? Hard to say. The locations are a little vague, but we know the relative ages: unconscious forces are far older than conscious forces. That's because—evolutionarily speaking— thinking is a fairly new thing.

Horses will not eat foxglove or tansy. No one told them the plants were poisonous. They don't have to 'think' about whether or not to eat them. They simply know better. That's an *instinct*, an *unconscious* process. People don't eat foxglove or tansy because we've been told the plants are poisonous, and we've been taught what poisonous means. That's *thinking*, that's a *conscious* process.

Although we thinking types are generally doing our darndest to ignore them, unconscious, instinctual forces are at work in us all the time. They spring from that vast colorful realm most of us reach only in dreams or drug-induced states, and they affect our waking lives whether we're willing to admit it or not. In fact, there seems to be some sort of direct psychological proportion along the lines of 'the less you can acknowledge the instinctual forces at work within you, the worse they'll act when they slip by your conscious guard.' *"I don't know what came over me."*

Classic fairy tales often begin with some sort of downward action. The hero or heroine gets lost in the woods, or falls from favor, or finds a stairway leading down into the earth, or is swallowed by a fish, or goes after a golden ball that rolled into a well. That's because human beings generally have to 'fall' to get anywhere. We're lazy. We don't change when all's well—we only change when we have to. We usually have to be *hurtin'* to change, which means **most real learning is preceded by suffering**. Most going forward entails leaving something behind.

Myths and hero tales follow the same format: 1) the hero, usually of divine or unusual parentage, ventures forth from his common world, 2) endures great suffering and hardship battling supernatural forces, and then, *by following his own heart,* 3) triumphs over what looked like insurmountable odds and brings a hard won gift back to the common world, which may or may not gladly receive the gift.[d]

Unfortunately, there's no getting around the suffering part. Suffering is vital to the enterprise. It's the hero's initiation. It's actually *the point*, it's the reason we tell all these stories over and over again. We're supposed to learn that overcoming obstacles by following your own heart makes one a hero. We're supposed to get that our fortunes are going to go up and down during this process, not just up and up, like the proverbial gross national product. We're supposed to realize that **dealing with dark times is necessary for the development of the human soul.**

So you see the problem here for us moderns. When *we* feel bad we usually reach for the remote. Or pop pills or drink something or smoke something or inject something or screw something. We don't like to feel bad, and we've seen enough advertising to convince ourselves that we shouldn't ever have to feel bad. But... if we don't let ourselves go 'down' into the depths occasionally, if we don't try to figure out *why* we feel bad and what we need to do about it, what will happen to heroism? Or learning? Or simply going forward?

If most real learning is preceded by suffering, then what's liable to happen to a society that absolutely refuses to analyze its own suffering? That panics at dark moods, rather than inquiring after their causes? What's liable to happen to a group of people who are so over-scheduled and over-stimulated they can't *hear* their own hearts? What are they going to learn?

How to buy things, apparently. Advertisements for anti-depressants on TV—as if they were just a product that anyone ought to have in the bathroom cabinet, like band aids or dental floss—are enough to *cause* depression. *{Of course anti-depressants can be useful in some cases. Nobody's arguing that. But as a first line of defense? For everybody? Without introspection or analysis or meditation? Shades of George Lucas' first movie 'THX'...}*

Dwelt on long enough, the irony here could cause more than depression— it could cause permanent brain damage. The USA prides herself on being the

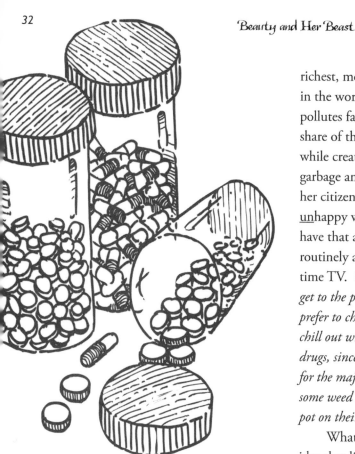

richest, most powerful country in the world. She devours and pollutes far more than her fair share of the world's resources while creating mountains of garbage and toxic waste. Yet her citizens are apparently so <u>un</u>happy with everything they have that anti-depressants are routinely advertised on prime time TV. ?? *{No wonder we can't get to the polls on election day. We prefer to chill out. And we prefer to chill out with the latest prescription drugs, since they're so profitable for the major companies, not with some weed anybody could grow in a pot on their back porch.}*

Whatever gave us the idea that life could proceed from birth to death without suffering, anyway? Ummm... advertisements for products designed to relieve suffering, most likely. With their constant barrage of happy/feely messages set to smarmy music: the adorable animals, *{who never pee or poop or chew up the furniture}* charming children and distinguished old folks who beam out at us from suburbia, the trucks that climb mountains, the impossibly gorgeous women, the incredibly hot men, the extremely cool graphics... not, of course, what any of us experience in real life, but... you see it often enough, you start expecting it to happen: happily ever after, right now. And not reached by soul searching, gaining wisdom, or developing character, either. Reached by *buying something*.

OK—that really *is* depressing. Pass the pills. No! **Back to the merchant!** who must have been relieved to stumble upon such a swanky looking palace in the middle of so dark a night. He didn't know how to get around in these woods, but by the looks of that castle, someone sure did. Someone with a lot of clout. Someone with vast resources and tremendous power.

And who's the best at getting around in the woods? Animals, of course— Beasts. Beasts aren't afraid of the dark. Beasts don't get lost in the woods. Beasts are right at home in the woods. They *need* the woods, they *use* the woods, for shelter and sustenance and protection.

Thus, to follow this metaphor, the less connection you have to your animal nature, the easier it is to get lost in the woods. The less you can recognize, or admit, or tap into, or benefit from that old instinctual nature of yours, the more it will scare you when it breaks through on its own.

Notice that no one forced the merchant into the castle. He wasn't kidnapped, or handcuffed, or blindfolded. He simply got tired of how things were going on the outside and went on in. Similarly, our own interior processes are open to us—well, some of them are, anyway—but unless we start 'losing our minds,' no one forces us to look inside. We have to *choose* to look within, consciously.

It's too bad, but the one thing you will not find advertised here in the USA is the way to do this: the way 'down.' Oh no, it's "Up!" always "Up!" that Americans are interested in. Despite the obviously circular nature of human life—birth, growth, maturity, decline, death—most of us just can't bear to think of it that way. We like linear. We like straight lines, please, and always going up. We don't *have* to mature, grow old, and die anymore. We just have to buy the right products.

So don't look for a lot of outside help in this area. There will be absolutely no 30 second spots advocating introspection during the Super Bowl. People don't stand around the water cooler at work discussing their dreams, nor do they hold discussions down at the tavern about how to plumb their creative depths. No one even *expects* anyone else to heed their own intuitions, much less follow their own hearts. That sort of behavior hurts productivity. It could cost you your job.

Do our elders throw a big celebration bash for us after we spend several days alone in the wilderness on our Coming-of-Age Vision Quest? No. *{Besides, the wilderness is now covered by a Wal-Mart super store and a couple of strip malls.}* In this culture, the way to get "down" underneath your conscious mind just isn't that clearly marked anymore.

These days, it's off the beaten path.

When the merchant awoke the next morning, he blinked in surprise to see a fine new suit laid out for him in place of his damp, dirty old one.

A kind fairy must own this castle, he thought. He looked out the window, and instead of a snow-covered wood, he saw masses of flowers blooming in the sun. Returning to the hall where he'd dined the night before, the merchant found a breakfast table set for one. "Kind fairy," he said aloud. "I am deeply obliged to you. Thank you for your generous care of me."

After a hearty breakfast, the merchant went outside to find his horse ready and saddled, and he set out for home at once. As he rode under a trellis covered with roses he thought of Beauty's wish, so he reached up and picked a rose for her.

Immediately there was a deafening roar, and a hideous Beast charged toward the merchant, snarling and growling. "Ungrateful man! I saved your life, I offered you hospitality, and then you steal my roses, my only pleasure, in return? Prepare yourself for death."

"Majesty, forgive me!" begged the merchant, dropping from his horse and falling to his knees. "I took the rose for one of my daughters."

"I am not a Majesty, I am a Beast!" roared the monster. "I know what I am, you wretched fool. Your flattery is pathetic, and your struggle would be useless.

"Yet you say you have daughters... if you have daughters perhaps you may live, merchant. If one of your daughters comes willingly to me in your stead, you may go free. I give you three months to decide. But know that, without fail, in three months, either you or one of your daughters must return to me."

The merchant had no thought of letting any of his children die for his sake, but as he wanted to at least see them one more time, he agreed to leave and return in three months.

"Then go now," said the Beast. "But I shall not leave your children penniless and orphaned over this folly of yours. There will be a trunk full of gold standing at your bedside by the time you reach your home."

What a strange Beast, thought the merchant, to be so cruel and yet so thoughtful at the same time. He left the castle, and now his horse seemed to know the way of its own accord, so he soon arrived at his own door.

But rather than filling him with joy, the sight of his children running toward him made him weep. As the merchant handed Beauty the rose he said, "Take this rose, Beauty. But little do you know what it cost your father."

Beastly Stuff

You can't stay in balance from way out on one end of the teeter-totter. 'Too good' does as much damage as 'too bad.' Being perfectly beautiful and perfectly sweet only makes Beauty's sisters perfectly jealous. Wanting nothing but a rose simply enrages the Beast. Again, the problems in this story are actually caused by Beauty, not by her sisters or the Beast.

But who—or what—is this Beast? A representative of the instinctual, animal aspect of human nature. Part of everyone, but far older than anyone—as old as the evolution of our species. As we can see from the story, he's rich and powerful and completely unpredictable, like nature herself: mild one minute, deadly the next. So understanding such a Beast can be difficult, as is calming him down if you rile him up.

The Beast lives in a hidden yet magnificent castle, not in some dank cave or crooked hut up on chicken's feet, and this is important symbolically. It means he knows how to live, and he lives well, but he's been removed from society. He was once a part of the human world, but lately he's fallen from grace. These days, unless someone seeks him out, the Beast can only hide in the woods and ambush the unwary—or sneak into town at night.

'Once upon a time' human beings were inextricably bound to the lives of animals and the world of nature. The intimate connections between human and animal, hunter and hunted, land and body, water and blood, were a part of daily life as well as the basis for ritual and ceremony. Many Native American cultures struggled valiantly to keep such traditions alive despite hordes of invading Europeans intent on wiping them out and taking their territory.

But in most places on the planet Earth, as civilization 'advanced,' as people spent more and more time developing complex hierarchical social systems—which run on thought at the expense of instinct—connections to the natural world and to animal instincts were weakened and pushed further and further from consciousness. Civilized people began to be ashamed of, and then finally to deny, any associations with animals or nature—other than exploitative. We began to think of ourselves as 'higher' than the animals. We began to think of nature as something fearful, needing to be tamed and conquered, not as something nurturing, to cooperate with.

In particular, Western civilizations developed religions that actually *refused* access to instincts and dreams and 'animal' impulses, on pain of eternal damnation. Pretty serious stuff, that eternal damnation. Fire and brimstone. So it's no wonder people became afraid of their Beasts. They could have been burned at the stake for embracing them. And plenty of them were.

In the words of our story, Western people started to get lost in the woods. The more civilized we became, the more we banished our animal and instinctual natures to the dark and stormy forests. Perhaps, as the poet and author Robert Bly speculates, it's inevitable.[c] Perhaps with each technological advance there's a necessary and corresponding spiritual loss. Perhaps each conscious gain has to push out some older unconscious entity, like knowing which plants are poisonous, in order to gain a toehold.

Who knows? What we *do* know is that microwaves cook so fast we get impatient now if it takes two minutes to boil water. We do know we can connect ourselves to the whole world via the Internet, as long as we focus on the monitor and don't look around the room we're in. We do know we can walk down the street talking to someone miles away through a telephone plugged into one of our ears *{Look ma, no hands!}* but only by ignoring the people right in front of us. We do know that unless

we're very careful from here on out, each technological advance will only make us more impatient with each living breathing moment, will only take us further away from the here and now which the instinctual nature calls home.

Most of us have simply stopped admitting—or thinking about, or listening to, or deciding what needs to be done for—our animal and instinctual natures. We've tried to banish our Beasts. *{I feel like picking on Descartes here—who came up with "Cogito Ergo Sum: I think, therefore I am"—but it's a little late to do any good, and he wasn't the only singer in that band anyway.}*

But has trying to banish our Beasts actually worked? Look at our movies. Look at our TV shows, our video games, our headlines, our endless wars—our obsession with guns and explosions and violence. Apparently banishment does *not* work. After several thousand years of conscious banishment, our *un*conscious Beasts are totally out of control and popping up everywhere.

Stories about sacrificing pure young maidens to hideous monsters are at least as old as written history. And there's a point lurking in there: ignoring monstrosity does not appease it. While we 'nice' people roam freely about our business up on the surface, the Beast imprisoned down in his labyrinth requires a steady diet of innocent victims. While we 'nice' people sing hymns of peace on Sunday and then go out to lunch afterwards, weapons explode in the faces of children in dusty villages so far away and so blasted by war and poverty that there's not potable water, much less restaurant food. Far away? How about those neighborhoods right on the other side of town, those neighborhoods "nice" people don't dare visit…

Bly poses some interesting questions: what if we asked the Beasts to stop hiding, to come up and join us? Could we forge a peace with them if we acknowledged their existence? Would they stop demanding human sacrifices if invited to a few classy dinner parties? Could we maybe even learn something from them?

How *do* they know which plants are poisonous, anyway?

When they'd heard their father's story the older girls howled and scolded and blamed Beauty. "Why could you not ask for clothes or jewels, as we did? Why do you have to be so wonderful? You've caused our father's death, yet you don't even shed a tear!"

"There's no need for tears," Beauty replied quietly. "The Beast said I could go in Father's place, and that's what I intend to do."

"No, sister!" cried her brothers. "We'll kill this monster, or perish in the attempt!"

"We cannot hope to kill him," said the merchant. "His power's far too great. I know you mean well, Beauty, but I am an old, old man, soon to die in any case. I only came back to bid you all good-bye."

But Beauty stood firm. "Father, I must go. I'd rather be eaten quickly by a Beast than die slowly from sorrow over causing your death."

And although the merchant tried in vain to reason with Beauty, she kept obstinately to her purpose. For their part, her sisters began to secretly rejoice at the thought of getting rid of her.

The merchant was so grieved he never once thought of the Beast's promise. Thus he was greatly surprised to find a chest full of gold coins standing by his bedside that evening. Bewildered, the merchant called Beauty, pointed to the open chest, and explained what the Beast had said to him.

"Good father," declared Beauty. "Two gentlemen have been courting my sisters in your absence. Use this money for their weddings."

Brothers like to fight

Beauty's brothers represent conscious masculine energy in this story, and they gladly offer to fight the Beast.

*{We need to stop and talk about the words masculine and feminine for a minute here: **symbolically** speaking, "consciousness, light, day, sun, intellect, dryness, etc." is masculine, and "unconsciousness, darkness, night, moon, instinct, moisture, etc." is feminine. It's not sexist, it's the way the symbols work in our minds, and have worked in our minds for thousands of years. **Whether you're male or female, your conscious processes are symbolically masculine and your unconscious processes are symbolically feminine.** There's no need to fret. It's not chauvinism. We've all got both, all the time.}*

Brothers like to fight. Whether it's an old story like *Bluebeard* or a new story like *Legends of the Fall*, the brothers gallop up with swords drawn and serious

expressions, ready to kick some butt.

In addition to fighting, conscious masculine energy tries to keep the Beast in line with rules, regulations and religions, which do not work any better than fighting does. Rules, regulations and religions just result in wars with those who have different rules, regulations and religions—or in crime.

These approaches are not ever going to work. You cannot beat the Beast by fighting, or by passing laws, or by calling him the devil. You can only beat the Beast by admitting he lives in your heart. If you can admit you have a Beast, right there in your own heart, then you can begin to tame him. Then you can teach him some manners.

There's definite value in the civilized, linear-thinking, heroic, masculine nature. Beauty's brothers don't hesitate a moment when courage is needed, or when sacrifice is called for. They're determined to do what's right at any cost. That's great. That's how we accomplish things in this world. That's the part of human nature that builds bridges and cures disease and eases suffering and puts food on the table. If we want public schools and safe roads and clean drinking water we have *got to* practice conscious decision-making.

But consciousness that walls itself off from its own instinctual processes is an orphan. It has no mother, no depth, no roots. Intellect needs contact with its animal nature for balance, for protection, for fierceness, for shrewdness—to be whole.

And wanting to use the gold for her sisters' weddings? There goes Beauty, right over the brink again, the little goody-goody. She's trying to buy her sisters off. She's trying to keep wickedness at bay by pretending it's not really wicked, when she should be looking squarely at the situation and meting out some justice.

Someone in touch with her animal, instinctual nature would not pretend everything was fine when she was looking at those two. She'd admit she had a problem and then do something about it. She wouldn't bare her neck, she'd defend herself. If Beauty were already in touch with her Beast, she wouldn't use that gold to pay for her sisters' weddings. She'd use that gold to hire a magician who could turn her sisters into toads.

But that'd be another story, wouldn't it.

Three months went by, only too fast. Then Beauty and her father made ready to set out for the Beast's castle. The two sisters rubbed their eyes with an onion to make believe they were crying, but the merchant and his sons cried in earnest. Only Beauty shed no tears. As the horses seemed to know the way, they reached the palace in a very few hours, where the horses went into the stable without bidding.

Inside the castle, Beauty and the merchant found a table for two set with gold plates, crystal glasses, and fine food. The merchant had very little appetite, but Beauty tried to be cheerful for her father's sake and began to eat, thinking, "I suppose the Beast means to fatten me up."

As they finished their supper they heard a great roar, and the Beast entered the room. Beauty was terrified, but she controlled her fear and sat still as he approached.

"Did you come here willingly?" growled the Beast, after looking at her for a long time.

"Yes," said Beauty.

"Then I am very much obliged to you. As for you sir," he said, turning to her father, "leave here tomorrow and do not even think of coming back. Good night, merchant. Good night, Beauty."

And with that, the Beast left them.

Choosing to seek the Beast

Now Beauty starts to be a little more likable. She stands up to her father and her brothers, shoulders the consequences of her actions, and starts off down her own road. Now she's not just "daddy's little girl" anymore, and such changes are usually more painful for the father who has to stay behind than they are for the daughter who gets to move forward. When the merchant cries in this passage, he may be crying for all the fathers who've been left behind by growing daughters.

For us civilized types, the first sight of a banished Beast *is* terrifying. We each have a personal unconscious that's as old as we are and develops as we develop, but our share of the collective unconscious is as old as human evolution. And just as the physical evolution of the human being can be traced in fossil records, the spiritual evolution of the human being can be traced by the things that appear in the collective unconscious.

This grab bag holds everything in our past: every god and every demon ever imagined, every blessing and every curse. Thus the collective unconscious is extremely juicy, but not at all tame. It's also far more emotional and far less logical than the newer 'civilized mind' we're so proud of, and its beastly parts are

starting to feel really pissed off about being repressed all these centuries. The results can be frightening, which might help to explain why Western religions began to insist the causes were 'out there,' "*The devil made me do it*," rather than 'in here,' as they are in Eastern religions.

But why is a Beast from a tough neighborhood like the collective unconscious being so well-mannered at the moment? He's "humbly obliged" to Beauty for coming to see him? Why doesn't he just rip her from limb to limb? Why's he being such a gentleman?

Because he *is* humbly obliged. Because the only legitimate way he could *get* to see her was if she came on over to his place. Here's this symbolism again: we're so civilized, we've become such able practitioners of conscious thought, that getting to instinctual material doesn't just *happen* anymore, not in a good way. We have to *make it* happen. Beauty and her father both chose to walk into the Beast's castle. The merchant sort of stumbled in, pushed by dire circumstances, so he may or may not learn anything, but Beauty is *choosing* to enter the castle of the Beast, even though she knows the Beast could eat her up. That's the hero's path.

To be eaten up is to disappear into, to be completely absorbed by, the eater. We fear we could get lost in nature. We're *told* we could get lost in nature. "*He just went wild.*"

So we stay away. We build thicker roofs and taller walls and bigger cities. We develop ever more elaborate indoor amusements. Until, as the centuries roll by, we gradually stop having anything to do with unreasonable old nature at all.

And—just as gradually—as the centuries roll by we lose our animal wisdom, our partnership with the planet we live on, our sixth sense, our cunning, our instinctual knowledge of which way to turn, our ability to see in the dark.

Then Beauty and her father said good night and went to bed, each expecting a sleepless night. Nevertheless, each immediately fell into a deep sleep.

Beauty dreamed of a beautiful lady who came to her and said, "Do not be afraid. Choose well, and you shall be rewarded."

As soon as they met the next morning, Beauty told her father about her dream.

And although it gave him some comfort, it was still a long time before Beauty could persuade her father to leave the castle.

A little background

Ah… at last! A mother figure. Who comes to Beauty in a dream, which is no accident. Dreams are one of the best routes to unconscious processes, and with no connection to her own mother, Beauty sorely needs the feminine input.

But why should Beauty have to get vital information from a fairy in a dream? Why *doesn't* Beauty have any connection to her own mother? Where *did* Mama go? To answer that, we need a short history of Western civilization. I'll paraphrase from two of Joseph Campbell's works, *The Power of Myth*,[f] and *Occidental Mythology*,[g] which is Volume III in his series *The Masks of God*.

What is now referred to as Western civilization was born in the great river valleys of the Nile, the Tigris-Euphrates, and the Indus. Circa 7500 to 3500 BCE, this was the territory of goddesses associated with agriculture and earthly cycles. A woman gives birth, just as the earth gives birth to plants. She gives nourishment, just as the earth gives nourishment. So in ancient Mesopotamia, the Egyptian Nile, and earlier planting cultures, womanly magic was associated with earthly magic. The goddess—from whom all things were born and to whom all things returned at death—was the prominent mythological form.

Beginning circa 4000 BCE, these agriculturally based, great mother cultures began to fall one after another to invading nomads—Semites and Indo-Europeans—who were herders and hunters. When one society takes another's territory, it either incorporates or annihilates the local gods, and installs its own deities as supreme beings. So as the agricultural societies fell to more warlike hunting and herding societies, the religions featuring goddesses who embraced all of creation went down one after the other, and the my-way-or-the-highway religions, featuring warlike gods with long lists of rules and very loud voices, rose up. When the Old Testament mentions "the Abomination," or people "worshipping on the mountaintops," right before it says to "kill every man, woman and child," it is referring to the old Canaanite goddess worshipers, and it is rationalizing the complete annihilation of their cultures by conquest.

Bloody conquests are the actual historical points where a symbol like the serpent sheds its skin. With these new warrior gods it was apparently not a good idea to ask questions, or to

desire to be as smart as they were. In fact, eating fruit from the Tree of Knowledge purchased a one-way ticket out of paradise. Curiosity, or the desire to know as much as the gods, became a punishable offense in Western thought somewhere right about here. Sort of explains one of the next big segments of Western history, doesn't it? **The Dark Ages.**

These victorious nomadic tribes eventually became Jewish, Christian and Muslim civilizations. Their religions were all influenced by the Persian Zoroaster (Zarathustra), who lived a thousand years before Christ and preached a strict *dualism* between god and man, good and evil. Zoroaster visualized a holy war between God (Ahura Mazda) and Satan (Angra Mainyu), and in his work we see the first glimmers of these later "solar monotheisms": religions with singular, warlike, all-powerful, totally masculine gods, viewed as separate from and completely 'above' humanity.

Their resulting societies were all extremely patriarchal in nature. Well, what did we expect? Under the more agricultural systems presided over by goddesses of nature and harvest, men and women worked together in ritual rounds of birth, growth, death and rebirth in a way described by the anthropologist Lucien Levy-Bruhl as "participation mystique."[h]

The reverence for the natural world and the levels of cooperation between sexes that existed in early fertile crescent societies—now confirmed by archaeological evidence—simply had to be eliminated for more aggressive societies to take over and establish complex power grids in which only a few were owners and all the rest were slaves. {See 'The Chalice and The Blade; Our History, Our Future,' for an overview of this archaeological evidence. Author Riane Eisler calls the earlier groups "partnership societies" and the later groups "dominator societies," and makes a thought provoking point: being stuck in "dominator" mode now doesn't mean we couldn't re-establish "partnership" societies in the future.[i]}

Or, as Erich Neumann rather poetically described it in The Origins and History of Consciousness, the nomadic warrior civilizations were struggling to leave the "womb" of unconscious participation in the world around them—a predominately feminine realm—for the "solar light" of conscious decision making—a predominately masculine realm.[j]

However, these victorious cultures did so in a peculiar and unprecedented way. Whereas Eastern religions were stressing the divinity within each individual—the traditional hands together Indian greeting "Namaste" actually means "the divinity within me salutes the divinity within you"—the Middle Eastern-into-Western religions were stressing obedience to a jealous, judgmental, masculine god outside of and completely separated from

themselves, reachable only through the proper hierarchical power channels. {We're bypassing a few side roads here—Greek rationalists, Jewish mystics, Gnostics, Alchemists, Troubadours, Renaissance—but if this is going to be a short history of Western civilization, we better stay on the main path.}

Thus, rather than being all-embracing, these emerging cultures stressed differences— god versus man, man versus nature, man versus woman, priest versus layman, black versus white, good versus evil, civilized versus primitive, winner versus loser, saint versus sinner, saved versus damned, us versus them—which is what dualism means, two—and, in the process, both the feminine principle and the natural world got the shaft.

Animals in these cultures were not revered as special beings—totems— with inherently valuable traits; they were property, to be herded and exploited. Women were not venerable participants in the great wheel of cosmic life— goddesses—any longer, nor were they even partners in everyday civic life any longer; they became villainous temptresses and/or collectible possessions.

Nature was not something to revere or cooperate with, nature—including human nature—was something to conquer and subdue.

And dreams? Well… if your 'hierarchical channel to God' stressed *never* having sexual relations, even with yourself, what would *you* dream about…? Dreams became the work of the devil, the last thing in the world a devout person should ever heed.

So it's no wonder that as these civilizations advanced, eventually covering all the land from Europe to India, it became far more important for a woman to be ladylike than to be in touch with her instincts. It became far more important for a woman to behave than to be powerful. In most situations it became flat dangerous for women to be powerful, or to follow their own hearts in any way, as it still is today in many parts of the 'civilized' world. Men—fathers, husbands, brothers, light, dry, solar—made the rules, and women—nurturing, instinctual, dark, moist, lunar—were supposed to obey them. Women were supposed to be good. Women were supposed to stay in the background and out of the decision making process, lest they be punished as witches and whores.

Thus, as we saw in the beginning of this story, Western civilization—that pinnacle of intellectual accomplishment which has now gone so far as to develop a wireless telephone—advanced at the expense of a connection to its own Mother: there's no one to call. By the time Jeanne-Marie Leprince de Beaumont wrote down this version of *Beauty and the Beast* in 1757, there was no mother at all for the six children, only a father.[k]

There were girls—good girls, naughty girls—but no grown women. Strong, grown-up women who participated equally in life with men—**along with all things wild, natural, uncanny, or instinctual**—had to be pushed way down out of sight, far down into the dark and stormy forests of the unconscious, for Western humanity's warrior-like, empire-building, conquesting-consciousness to emerge.

The beautiful lady in the dream is telling Beauty, "Enough with the one-sidedness already! We can start making better choices than this now. Let's start using both sides of the yo-yo again!"

She's telling Beauty to cherish her animal, instinctual nature. She's telling Beauty it's perfectly OK to follow her heart and heed her dreams.

She's telling Beauty—that sweet, good, innocent, well-educated, upper-class specialist in classical music and polite conversation—to choose what appears to be a Beast as a mate.

After her father had gone, Beauty wandered through the castle. Each spot seemed more beautiful than the next, until she came to a door which said, "Beauty's Room." It opened to reveal a suite far more splendid and tasteful than any of the rest. What amazed her most was a large library filled with artwork, books, musical instruments, and sheets of music. *Why does the Beast take such pains to amuse me if he means to eat me up?* she thought. She opened one of the books and saw written in gold letters on the frontispiece -

Beauteous lady, dry your tears,
Here's no cause for sighs or fears.
Command as freely as you may,
For you command and I obey.

"Then I wish to know what my father is doing right now," said Beauty. Immediately the looking glass on a nearby table held a picture of her home, with her father riding mournfully up to the door. She watched as her brothers and sisters ran out to meet him, and then the image faded away as fast as it had appeared.

Beauty felt sorely puzzled that the Beast, who was so frightening, and hideous, and powerful, could also be so thoughtful, and generous, and kind.

The personal shadow

Well, that *is* the puzzle, isn't it? We want things to be black or white, good or evil, for us or against us—a "function of Biblical thinking," Campbell observed—but it's just not that easy. People are complicated. Life is complicated. The simplest human impulse stems from gnarled and ancient roots. There is no one way to act that can be worn around like a suit of armor and used in every situation. Every archetype—every instinctual impulse of human nature—has a value and a use. *{And a danger.}* Sometimes I'm the goddess of wisdom, sometimes I'm the village idiot.

If an accident happens right in front of you and simple physical strength on your part will save someone's life, you'll become as strong as a giant in an instant, without even thinking about it. You'll lift up that rock or pull the door off that car, no problem. But since giants are dumb as stumps and extremely boorish, you'll push your giant offstage and call up your prince charming before the TV crews arrive. By the time a newsperson sticks a microphone in your face you'll be your normal strength again, polite and well spoken. There's an entire *cast* of archetypes milling around inside each one of us, just longing for a chance to go on stage. The entire cast of myth and tale and dream stands waiting in the wings of our psyches.

However, we human beings tend to get stuck in one role. We generally learn these roles in our family theatre, and then continue to play them out in the world at large. We don a certain mask every day and go out and perform "I'm cute," or "I'm cool," or "I'm smart," or "I'm a victim" or what*ever*, day after day

after day, just as if we *were* characters trapped in fairy tales. Unless knocked off balance by a disaster of some sort, we tend to muddle along all through life stuck in one persona.

Look at poor Beauty: kind, long suffering, beautiful and dutiful. Now *there's* a limited role. And how could such a role possibly be sustained for a human lifetime? Could a girl like this ever admit she'd been mean, or told a lie? Could she ever admit she farted, or felt horny? Could she simply own up to being in a bad mood? Of course not! This woman is perfect.

So if she were human, and dedicated to performing a 'Beauty' of a role like this, her options would be limited. She could push a bad mood way down into the forbidding forest of her unconscious, denying she knows anything at all about it, and/or, she could blame her bad moods on someone else.

Carl Gustav Jung, one of the 'big three' fathers of modern psychoanalysis (Freud, Jung, Adler) first coined the term "human shadow."[1] *{As well as introvert, extrovert, and complex. He was also the first to try to determine which basic psychological processes a person tends to use the most, which has evolved into the Myers-Briggs type tests used by many employers today.}*

Jung used the word "shadow" to describe the parts of a human being that the person doesn't want to, or can't, think about or acknowledge. It refers to the repressed, unlived side of your normal daytime personality—the stuff you don't like about yourself, the stuff you don't want anyone to know about you.

Thus your shadow contains negative qualities, such as envy or prejudice or insecurity. Or it could even contain positive qualities, such as compassion or artistic ability. But the qualities, whatever they are, stay in your shadow because you don't like to—in fact most of the time you simply *can't*—admit you possess them. Some parts of ourselves we like to show to others—put out into the light—and some parts of ourselves we like to hide—keep in the shadows.

The word 'shadow' was a stroke of genius. It gives us a mythological way of looking at a common psychological problem, and symbolically it is a very good fit. Your shadow can't be smelled or tasted or touched or felt, yet it is actually hooked to you, attached to the creases and crevices and neurons of your daylight mind. And while other people can see your shadow without too much trouble, you usually have to turn your head around to see it.

There's also a nifty paradox built into both meanings of the term: whether it's a shadow cast by light in the natural world, or a shadow cast by your mind, **the brighter the light shines, the darker the shadow it creates.** The vilest acts in history have been done—and are still being done right this minute—in the name of God, which is the brightest light imaginable.

The enchantments and bewitchments which

occur in fairy tales are reminders. Warnings. Because most of us fall into an enchantment at one time or another. We misunderstand the stories. We think we need to *be* Beauty, or *be* a hero, so we stick ourselves into that role and try *not* to be anything else.

We just get stuck. In the process of trying to fit into our role—as athlete or honor student or devoted disciple or skinny woman or powerful businessman or respectable wage earner or laidback dude or hardened gang member—we deny the very existence of any part of ourselves that doesn't fit neatly into that role. We deny we have any desire to skip class or eat the whole bag of cookies or blow off work today or hop into bed with a total stranger.

And we usually can manage to cram all those contrary desires way down into our shadows. *"What contrary desires? I don't see any."* That is, until we wake up one day and find ourselves doing something *really* stupid and totally *"out of character."* Out of character... out of the role we've chosen—or were assigned—to play. Which was probably a fairy tale character's role, from a fairy tale family, in a fairy tale setting, and not humanly possible in the first place. It's poignant—and poisonous and highly paradoxical—that despite the evil increasing exponentially around the world, most of us are trying so hard to be good.

Denying real parts of your psyche—and that word means *soul*—on a daily basis is called repression, and it creates another ongoing problem called regression. If I can't admit I even have certain feelings, if they shame me, or they scare me, or if my culture won't permit them, so I hide them down in my shadow for a few decades, those feelings are not going to look the same when they get past my conscious guard at some point in mid-life. They will have regressed.

Re-gress is the opposite of pro-gress. To regress is "to go backwards." The parts of myself I just can't stand to admit will get *less* human the longer I ignore them. The longer I pretend not to know anything at all about some part of myself, the grosser and coarser and hairier and wilder that abandoned part of myself is going to get, like a troll living under a bridge, or a castaway all alone on an island.

What makes a bunch of good ole boys who usually hang out down at the café go out and lynch a black man? Or beat a gay man to death and leave his body dangling from a barbed wire fence? What makes one commuter pull out a gun and shoot another commuter over an insignificant driving mistake? Who does the actual torturing in a torturous regime? Were these people all *born* evil?

No. No one is born evil. However, we are all capable of a distinct downward slide as we move through life—from repression, to regression, to aggression.

When we're never less than angelic on the surface, the devil inside dances. When we have no idea what we feel, and wouldn't admit it if we did; when we simply cannot admit being wrong; when we think we have to have it together at all times—that's self-enchantment. That's being firmly stuck in a fairy tale role.

And there's only one way to break such an spell: to take off the mask.

To face the fact that every person on earth—you, me, and the guy in the corner booth over there—is just as much Court Jester as Wise King, just as much Wicked Witch as Snow White.

To go ahead and admit we're not always perfect, so we can start to do something toward mending our mistakes.

In the middle of the day Beauty found a table elegantly set for one. A delightful concert played all during her luncheon, but not a soul could she see. Finally, at dinnertime, she heard the noise of the Beast approaching.

"Beauty," he growled, "may I stay while you eat dinner?"

"As you wish. You are master here," she answered.

"No!" said the Beast. "In this place you alone command. If you don't want my company, you need only to say so, and I'll leave on the instant. Am I very ugly to you, Beauty?"

"Why, yes," said she. "But you can also be very considerate."

"Yes, I can," replied the Beast sadly. "Yet, still I am an ugly, stupid Beast."

"Well, not stupid," laughed Beauty. "Stupid people are never aware of their own stupidity."

At this the Beast looked pleased, but only managed to say, "Please don't let me keep you from your dinner, and be sure you're well served. Consider all you see as your own. I should be deeply grieved if you lacked for anything."

"Your kindness makes me forget how ugly you are," replied Beauty. "Truly, many men are more beastly than you. A handsome heart and an ugly face are far better than a handsome face and an ugly heart."

"I'm too stupid to reply properly," the Beast growled. "But thank you for your good opinion."

Then they spoke of many things, and Beauty had almost forgotten to be afraid of him when the Beast turned to her and asked abruptly, "Beauty, will you marry me?"

She sat awhile, shocked and silent. Then at last she simply said, "No, Beast."

At which the Beast sighed, said "Good night, Beauty," and left her.

The national shadow

While there's no denying that the unconscious mind has many interesting and powerful channels, in our day and age the conscious mind has the remote. Beauty usually does rule, and the Beast usually does try to obey. If we want our

animal nature to disappear, that's what it has to try to do. If we want to pretend we're always nice, then our bad actors have to sneak around to get out. *{That's a Robert Bly line: "If we want to pretend we're always nice, then our bad actors have to sneak around to get out." ⁽ᵐ⁾ And it's a pretty nifty one-sentence synopsis of the entire civilized situation, if you think about it for a while. The old poet.}*

The Beast is unsatisfied with such a lop-sided dominance. He yearns for a 'marriage,' a union. Beauty may rule the way things are, but the Beast is still a Beast, and Beauty is still his prisoner. He knows neither of them will get anywhere near 'happily ever after' until

there's a 'marriage;' until instinct and intellect join forces.

We can give Beauty some more credit here, though. She continues to wise up. People can definitely act like beasts, and the less capable they are of admitting their beastliness, the more beastly they tend to act.

That's because shadow material is cunning. Your shadow is part of your psychological make-up, which means it has to, it *will*, show up somewhere in your life. Unfortunately, you can't avoid running into parts of yourself. So if there are things you just can't stand to admit about yourself, if you just can't face some of your own stuff, then you're going to see your own stuff on someone else's face.

Guaranteed. It's not going to disappear. It won't give up and go away and leave you alone merely because you don't want to think about it. It will keep popping up here and popping up there until it gets your attention—like those banished beasts who required periodic victims—and those *other* people that you *can* see doing it will look worse and worse to you as time goes on.

Let's say I'm acting like a monster: all pissed off for no discernible reason. Maybe I'm stomping around blaming whatever's happening to me on someone else—despite the fact that I'm actually doing it myself right at that very moment. Or maybe I'm muttering under my breath about how out of it some *other* person is, without being able to hear how out of it *I* sound. But I don't see (or hear) what I'm doing. I don't stop to wonder where all this muttering is coming from, or what such a habit says about me, or make an effort to snap out of it, and I certainly don't look for a solution to whatever problem I'm muttering about.

Hell, no. I just 'blame on' until I run out of steam. Like it's OK. Like it doesn't matter. Like it's not important. And hey, it's totally normal anyway. Everybody does it. If someone I wanted to impress came over I could always cover up my muttering monster with a big ole smile. After all, he doesn't have a thing to do with me. He's not even real.

Or, maybe I don't actually do my own muttering. Maybe I just tune in to the right stations so I can gloat when I hear someone else say really monstrous things—maybe I let a talk show host do my dirty work. If this eternal belly-aching, fault-finding, fact-twisting, finger-pointing and shockingly-unfair-running-down-of-those-who-deign-to-disagree-with-me is only coming from talk show hosts, then I'm not really a monster, am I? Just because I tuned in to those stations?

Ah… yeah—afraid I am. Monsters aren't that easy to disown. Monsters are just as pathetically desperate for attention as everything else in my shadow. In fact, monsters are so pathetically desperate for attention that **the longer I pretend I never have any monstrous thoughts myself, the more people around me will start to look and sound like monsters.**

Kind of explains why we hear so much ranting and raving over the airways, doesn't it? Why it's so easy for us to get all hot and bothered about what someone *else* is doing… why we just can't seem to get off certain subjects…

It's pretty simple really: **we dwell on what other people are doing so we don't have time to think about what we're doing ourselves.**

This is called projection, in psychological terms, and it happens all the time. It starts with denial, and ends in blame. We take some part of ourselves we don't like—or are ashamed of, or don't want to think about, or can't bring ourselves to deal with—and project it out onto another person, where we can see it. Imagine a movie projector. You would be the projector whirring in that little room at the back, and the other person would be the big screen down in front. You're *creating* the image, but the other person is the only place where you can *see* the image.

Thus we can hate that *other* person for having whatever awful quality we're projecting, while remaining steadfastly in love with ourselves and not having to change a thing. "*I don't have a bad temper. What are you talking about, you asshole? You have a terrible temper!*"

Now it gets serious. I'm sure you've heard that Denial ain't just a river in Egypt. Well, Projection and Blame ain't just small towns in Texas. We are not talking about a quaint practice only carried out by a few remote primitives somewhere on the other side of the planet. This cycle—**denial-projection-blame**—is a basic psychological mechanism. This is a description of what went on at your dinner table last night. This is a description of what we each do all day long unless we're making a sincere effort not to do so, and probably a good 78.87% of the time even then.

There's no getting around the fact that human beings are now using their intelligence to project whatever they don't like about themselves onto other people, rather than using their intelligence to correct whatever it is about themselves they don't like. Shoot—we're *taught* to project whatever we don't like about ourselves onto other people. Children hear their parents and teachers and leaders do it every day. Hang out in any schoolyard, anywhere in the world, for one whole recess period, and count how many times one kid blames another kid for what he or she just did. Where do they learn that?

Start looking around for the human shadow. It won't take you long to find it—in history, in current politics, in the news, in the paper, on the radio, on television, in your own home, and in your own heart. Nor will it take you long to come to the conclusion that this is not some harmless procedure easily overlooked among friends. This is one of humanity's biggest problems.

As Bly put it, *"Projection of shadow material causes most of the misery, injustice and warfare in the world."* [n]

And as Jung wrote, *"Learning to integrate shadow material is the single most important task facing mankind, as failure to do so will lead to the extinction of the human race."* [o]

Whoa. What? Extinction of the human race? What the hell is he talking about? Why'd he say that?

Because we not only project blame individually, we project blame as whole cultures. Or, *whole cultures have shadows.*

A hat that looks really cool in a bar in Wyoming may not look cool at all on Fifth Avenue in New York. There are substantial cultural differences between the Pacific Northwest and the Deep South. Between being German or Sudanese. Between Chinese and Chilean. We're not just 'stuck' in ego roles and family roles; we're stuck in social-historical-mythological eras and areas. And then, in practice, we refine our differences even further by only hanging

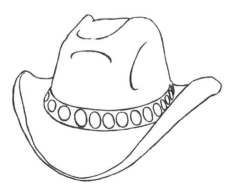

out with people *inside* our era and area who are the most like us. Red State, Blue State.

As history has shown over and over again, if enough people deny and project the same qualities something really nasty can occur: like Inquisitions, or exterminations of native populations, or slavery, or the Third Reich, or Israelis and Palestinians, or Shiites and Sunnis, or genocide, or Corporate America, Where the Rich Get Richer! while everyone else gets laid off without access to health care. **Massive acts of evil simply cannot be perpetrated without massive amounts of denial, projection, and blame.**

It works this way because the human shadow comes in layers, as does the unconscious mind. There's a personal layer and a collective layer. Thus we each have a *personal shadow* that can get out of hand—for example, making fun of how other people look when we're insecure about our own attractiveness. Then, in addition to the personal shadow, we each participate in a *collective shadow* that can get out of hand—for example, accusing another group of evil when we can't bear to look at the evil our own group has done.

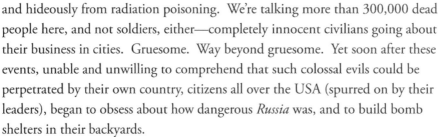

An excellent example of this occurred in US history at the end of WWII. After the saturation bombing of German cities by British and US forces which culminated in a firestorm at Dresden so fierce it literally melted 100,000 people, the USA dropped two atomic bombs on a country that was *trying to surrender* to the Allied forces.ᴾ At Hiroshima and Nagasaki 150,000 people were killed instantly, and tens of thousands later died slowly and hideously from radiation poisoning. We're talking more than 300,000 dead people here, and not soldiers, either—completely innocent civilians going about their business in cities. Gruesome. Way beyond gruesome. Yet soon after these events, unable and unwilling to comprehend that such colossal evils could be perpetrated by their own country, citizens all over the USA (spurred on by their leaders), began to obsess about how dangerous *Russia* was, and to build bomb shelters in their backyards.

I grew up with one of those bomb shelters in my backyard. *{No lie: there was an actual bomb shelter built on our property in Fort Worth, Texas, in the 1950s. At first it was all clean and full of water and canned goods, later it got dirty and full of spider webs and snakes, and then finally, after many years of neglect, my Aunt Eddie planted iris all over it, so it eventually became a little hill of flowers with a hollow core.}* I also grew up hearing stories about how brutal *the Japanese were* in WWII.

In other words, there is a 'me against you' aspect to the personal shadow, and there is an 'us against them' aspect to the collective shadow. And projected out onto others, both types of shadow material harm—do actual damage to—the targets of their projections. Not just psychic mumbo-jumbo, real harm. "Bombs in the baby carriages," as Paul Simon said in *Graceland*.[q]

Politicians manipulate us by pulling the strings to our collective shadow ties; by using symbols and symbolic language, which stimulate the unconscious. Even if my party just lost an election, or I'm totally irate at what the USA is up to, I cannot hear the *Star Spangled Banner* without getting tears in my eyes. It just gets me, every time, at a deep emotional level.

The truth is, we each have to belong to something bigger than ourselves to make it on this planet, and the scarier this planet gets, the more we unconsciously hope whatever we belong to is really powerful. Mighty. Right. Beyond reproach. So we all respond heartily—no thinking necessary—to waving flags, old familiar tunes, catchy slogans, or links to the past through the use of archetypal words like 'fatherland' or 'motherland' or 'homeland.' Hitler was a consummate master of the symbol. The salute, the swastika, the rows upon rows of clean uniformed youths singing and marching in step… symbols like these speak directly to the need to belong to, and be protected by, something bigger than ourselves that dwells in every human heart.[r]

Political examples of the collective shadow abound. We're going to look at an "evil empire" example, since it's completely transparent yet frequently used. But before we do, two things need to be stressed:

1) We are not just talking about Republicans or Democrats here, nor are we just talking about the USA. We're talking about how the shadow side of human nature operates on a massive scale. If it feels like I'm picking on the USA, that's because I live in the USA and what my country does matters to me. But go ahead and choose any other country you want. Look into it and you'll find the same thing: denial, projection and blame, operating on colossal scales.

2) This will not be easy reading for most people in the USA. We'd all like to believe the surface version of the fairy tale. We'd all like to live without guilt in the home of the free and the brave. But projecting shadow material on a national level is serious, deadly business. We all also need to get beyond our unconscious dependencies on fantasy scenarios so we can deal responsibly with the realities of life.

So… an example of the national shadow at work in politics: *in a 2002 State of the Union Address,* a President of the United States called three *other* countries an *"axis of evil"* for "selling arms to enemies" and "fostering terrorism."

Perfect… who produces and sells more arms than any other country in the world? Why the USA, of course. And what was 'Iran-Contra'? Oh, that was when the USA not only *sold arms to an enemy* that was holding US citizens hostage at the time—Iran—it then *used the profits from those illegal sales to secretly train and finance a guerilla army*—the Contras—which *overthrew* a legitimately elected government in Nicaragua. What was the President accusing those *other* countries of? Was it selling arms to enemies and fostering terrorism… ?

This is an example of "the pot calling the kettle black." Like name calling on the playground, except with far deadlier ammo. And while it does let off a little saber-rattling steam and allow the USA to feel superior for the moment, blasting other governments in public speeches will not solve any of the USA's problems. It will not provide universal health coverage, balance the budget, adequately fund education, hold corporations accountable to their cultures, lower our dependence on fossil fuels, or index the minimum wage to the cost of living.

That's one of the problems with slinging shadow material around. It doesn't get a damn thing done except damage. It's just subterfuge. The more we accuse others of, the more we can get away with ourselves—the best defense is a good offense. What George Orwell called "doublethink" and "newspeak" in his famous novel *1984.*[5]

Wow. Here's a handy coincidence: the radio was playing in the background while I sat here typing, and when I realized the President of the United States was speaking, I stopped to listen. Amazing. I was sitting here trying to think of how to explain the human shadow at a national level, and an example came wafting in over the air waves to enter the pages of this book on its own accord.

This morning the President spoke to a crowd in Tbilisi, Georgia, about the glories of "freedom" and "democracy." He gave a homey, heart warming, cliché-filled, archetype-stirring speech. I listened to the whole thing, which sounded great. Very presidential. I was impressed, particularly by the way it would have been impossible to disagree with a word he said: I mean, who *doesn't* love freedom or democracy? And of course the speech was... all doublethink, all newspeak.

As the genie said to Aladdin, let's "Wake up and smell the hummus!" This particular president was not democratically elected *himself.* He was appointed by his father's appointees to the Supreme Court and his brother's State Election Officials on the first go-round, and he only managed to be re-elected for a second term by continually 'misrepresenting' the facts and smearing his opponent's character. He's not practicing democracy, he's participating in a corporate dynasty that does whatever it wants. And trumpeting the glories of "freedom" and "democracy" in folksy speeches will not change nor hide the facts: his administration destroyed a sovereign government in Iraq for false reasons, in defiance of world opinion, unleashing bloody chaos.

So—what is such a man *doing* when he uses the words "freedom" and "democracy" over and over in a speech? *{Doublethink.}* Trying to fool the rest of us? *{Newspeak.}* Trying to convince himself? *{Delusion.}* For that matter, what do the words "freedom" and "democracy" mean used by any President of the United States?

Is "democracy" when the USA overthrows another legitimately elected government leader—like Allende in Chile, or Arbenz in Guatemala, or Mossadegh in Iran—for not playing along with her corporate schemes to fleece their country of resources? Or is "democracy" when the USA installs and supports an appallingly abusive dictatorship where nobody gets a vote—like Pinochet in Chile, or Armas in Guatemala, or the Shah in Iran—because it *will* play along with her corporate schemes to fleece their country of resources?

And what is "freedom"? Is "freedom"

what happened to the Africans we enslaved and the
Native Americans who were here first? Is "freedom"
what happens right now down in Gitmo?

As long as I'm waxing rhetorical with the
questions here, can the lofty words being used
in this President's speech today be stretched high
enough to embrace the Roldos/Torrijos coincidence?
These men were both elected, charismatic, reform-
minded Central American presidents who had the
effrontery to feel that a country's resources should
be used primarily for the good of its own people—
Jaime Roldos in Ecuador, and Omar Torrijos in
Panama—and they *each died mysteriously in fiery
plane crashes within two months of one another* back
in 1981. Hugo Chavez, Evo Morales—watch your
backs.

Please read *A People's History of the United States*, by Howard Zinn.[i] It just
might change your life. And while you're at it, read *Confessions of an Economic
Hit Man*, by John Perkins,[ii] as well as *Overthrow*, by Stephen Kinzer, quoted
below.[v] It's time we did a little homework. It's time we bumped ourselves
out of this knee-jerk, for-me-or-against-me, flag-waving-without-thinking-
patriotism, which can be so easily exploited by politicians.

The sad fact is: the USA has fostered more terrorism in more different
places than any other country in recent history—whether a Democrat *or* a
Republican was in the White House. **Fourteen** other governments have been
deposed by the USA since 1893:

"*Throughout the twentieth century and into the beginning of the twenty-first,
the United States repeatedly used its military power, and that of its clandestine
services, to overthrow governments that refused to protect American interests. Each*

*time, it cloaked its intervention in the rhetoric of national security
and liberation. In most cases, however, it acted mainly for
economic reasons—specifically, to establish, promote, and defend
the right of Americans to do business around the world without
interference.*"[w]

The word "covert"—which we hear all the time in
reference to our own policies—does not happen to mean
"above board." It happens to mean secret, under the table,
clandestine, guerilla—terrorist. So how hypocritical is
it, what heights of doublethink and newspeak have we

reached, to be the country proclaiming a "War on Terrorism?"

And while it's slightly understandable that we swallow whatever we hear or don't hear from our leaders without question—because we want our country to be right at all times, and are thus willing to ignore evidence to the contrary— how should we *expect* those who are being oppressed and bereaved by our policies to feel? Happy for us? Ready to turn the other cheek? Not at all interested in revenge? *{Whew. End of questions.}*

We need to snap out of it, fellow citizens of the USA. Announcing a "War on Terrorism" and taking our shoes off at the airport will not keep us free from harm. And it would not keep us free from harm even if it were actually possible to shoot, bomb or imprison all the people all over the world who ever wanted to perform a terrorist act against us. *{…Imagine that. Talk about '1984'…}*

Unless the USA changes her conduct, a "War on Terrorism" will be an endless, futile, unspeakably tragic expenditure of lives and loyalties without the slightest hope of victory. That is a very bleak scenario, and the reason behind it is simple cause and effect: as long as a powerful country—**any powerful country**—gives noble sounding speeches while actually performing nefarious acts, people in the afflicted countries can't help but hate her. No matter how eloquently her leaders *talk* about noble sounding ideas like democracy or freedom, those being exploited and oppressed will still know—to the depths of their beings, from their own history and experience—that profits of ruling corporate dynasties are valued far more highly than their own lives.

This is not exactly news, folks. Hell—it's the oldest story in the world, and we already know how it ends. The Greeks called it **hubris**: that great, overweening pride that feels invincible, can't get enough of itself, and thus causes its own fall. Hindus and Buddhists have an idea called **karma**: that people are bound to experience the type of action they commit. Christians say: **you reap what you sow**. Hippies used to say: **what goes around comes around**.

Whatever you want to call it, there is a price to pay for projecting shadow material on a national scale. My mind keeps seeing those towers explode, one after the other, in New York City. Or it counts the dead and maimed coming back from Iraq. Or it dwells on a fun loving friend of mine from high school— now a sad and shattered alcoholic—who will never get over the fact that he killed children in Vietnam.

Projection—on any scale—works because it's easier to see the faults in others than it is to see the faults in ourselves.

It's easier to accuse others of beastliness than it is to accept our own beastliness.

It's easier to think someone else is wrong than it is to be wrong.

It's simply much easier to blame someone else than it is to change.

Personally *or* collectively.

We'd really like to believe all the monsters are on the outside.

But, just like Beauty said, the real monsters are on the inside.

Personally *and* collectively.

Makes them hard to see.

Three quiet months passed. Each night the Beast came while Beauty ate dinner. Each day he proved his kindness. The only sad moment came in the evening, as the Beast always asked, "Beauty, will you marry me?" before he left her, and Beauty always had to refuse.

One night she added, "You're very dear to me, Beast. I shall always be your friend. But I shall never be able to marry you."

"You're my only joy, my only reason for living," the Beast begged in return. "I'd die without you. At least promise you'll never leave me."

And Beauty blushed deeply, for that very day the mirror had revealed that her father lay ill, sick with worry, close to death. She'd been longing to go and comfort him.

"Beast, I promise never to leave you for good. But I want to visit my father. My sisters are married, my brothers are in the army, and my father is left all alone, worrying and grieving over me. Let me go and stay with him for a week and comfort him."

"Go, then," the Beast answered stiffly. "Go to your father's house tonight. And you will stay there, and I will die here of grief."

"No, Beast!" cried Beauty. "I would never be the cause of your death. I promise to return in a week."

"You'll wake at home tomorrow," said the Beast. "When you want to come back here, just put this ring on the table as you go to bed. Good night, Beauty."

And the Beast sighed an even deeper sigh than usual as he left her.

It may be nasty, but we gotta deal with it

We normally *don't* want to marry our virtuous maiden to our hideous monster. It's hard to love the parts of ourselves that we feel are beastly, that we've been told are nasty, much less decide to settle down and raise a family with them. We're normally ashamed and afraid of our Beasts. That's why we keep them in our shadows.

In order to make our parents happy we started hiding parts of ourselves before we could walk. And we definitely knew the difference between approval and disapproval before we could talk. It's another basic survival skill. We can't make it on our own as infants. We have to depend on the goodwill of others. So if we hear we're too much trouble, or our poop stinks, or we're too chubby or too clingy or too loud, we learn to stuff those parts down into our shadows very quickly. By second grade, hiding parts of ourselves in order to please others has become second nature.

Which is not a totally bad thing. In order to become a thinking human being who can cooperate with other thinking human beings, some of that old animal instinctual nature needs to be controlled. Some parts of the psyche are like Beauty's sisters: only out for themselves. "Letting it all hang out" is not a viable option among intelligent mammals who've been honing their warfare skills in dominator societies for thousands of years.

But we do have a responsibility to deal with the things we keep in our shadows as frankly and honestly as we can before they get so desperate for attention they sneak out on their own. What was that Bly line? "If we want to pretend we're always nice, then our bad actors have to sneak around to get out."

Yeah. If we refuse to admit that we even have certain feelings, we exclude the possibility of dealing with those feelings rationally. If we don't accept responsibility for our own shadow, we set everyone else around us up for ambush by whatever we left lurking in there. Like *Dr. Jekyll,* who was such a perfect specimen of culture and civility that he spent most of his time helping those less fortunate than himself, and his alter ego *Mr. Hyde,* who snuck out at night to persecute prostitutes and prey on the weak.[x]

There's a recurring theme in animal husband stories—and literature in general—about taming the Beast, about soothing the savage soul. But for that to happen, someone in the story has got to pay attention to the poor old Beast. In the outer world, no creature thrives on neglect, no critter likes a cage. It's the same in the inner world: **any archetypal character prowling around in your psyche will act better and be easier to handle if you can (1) admit that it exists, and (2) find out what it wants.** Then you can open negotiations with it.

Let's go back to selfishness. We have a good strong image for that in Western folklore—a dragon hunched over his hoard. Now these dragons never actually *use* the treasure they steal. They just hoard it. Take it from others, pile it up in a cave somewhere, and lie around on it. Breathe fire. Eat whole cows and coy maidens.

Can I better manage my internal dragon by pretending not to be selfish, *"I'm not being selfish. I deserve a bigger piece than you do."* or by keeping an eye out for my selfishness? And when I do catch myself being selfish, could I just admit

it, maybe even laugh at myself as I see it happening? *"Geez, look at that. Cut my piece of pie a lot bigger than yours, didn't I? I'm such a rascal. Here, let me divvy this up better."*

That might work. But if I go around trying to pretend I'm not being selfish, I'm never going to be able to *stop* being selfish. I'm never going to have an accurate picture of what I'm actually doing, or of who I really am, plus I'll have a lousy sense of humor. Where it starts to get ugly is: I'm going to have to keep other people distracted, probably by accusing them of something first, so they'll be too busy defending themselves to notice how much bigger I just cut my own piece of pie. What a lot of work for a little more dessert! And, of course, the chance to appear free from all flaws—so important in a black and white, either/or, judgmental culture.

My old dragon of selfishness will simply get bigger and greedier the longer I pretend not to know anything about him. Left alone without recognition or supervision, he will eventually get big enough to swoop out over the countryside torching people and taking whatever he wants. And he will always have good, solid reasons for doing so if caught or questioned. The dragon of selfishness can morph into the angel of justification in an eyeblink.

But if I can manage to look inside once in a while and admit he's in there, say, *"Oh, there you are. I see you, you greedy old thing,"* maybe throw him a nice little steak or buy him a new pair of shoes, my dragon will settle down and go back to sleep. If I allow him a little conscious space, he won't have to torch or steal or drive like a maniac or cheat on exams or embezzle company funds to get my attention.

The Beast resorts to begging in this part of the story because he's well aware that the beastly parts of a human being cannot be ignored, walled off, denied, or blamed on someone else without getting *more* beastly. If he loses Beauty's attention now, he loses the best parts of himself—"I shall die." So if he can't get her to marry him, he at least wants to know she'll stay somewhere near him, that he won't be pushed out of her sight, exiled from consciousness—her father's house—forever.

Her father's house... at the beginning of this story Beauty lived totally within her father's house. She spent all her time with him, and there was no mention of a wife for him or a suitor for her. Now we're seeing a definite maturation in Beauty's outlook toward her father. Now she's talking about visiting Dad, but living elsewhere. Now she has a suitor, even if he could use a shave.

There's always more than one thing going on in a classic fairy tale, just as there's always more than one thing going on in a myth or a dream or a work of art. No one interpretation is ever "it," no one look can exhaust the view. Fairy tales, like myths and dreams and works of art, speak symbolic language, and symbols are infinite, inexhaustible. They open out, or perhaps that should read, they open "in." Symbols refer beyond themselves to the big ideas, the ones which cannot be adequately expressed in words.

This book stresses the shadow aspects of *Beauty and the Beast* because I'm obsessed with getting the concept of the human shadow out into the world so people can start using it. Someone else analyzing *Beauty and the Beast* might have a different focus. They might choose to dwell on how necessary it is for a woman to break cleanly away from her father in order to have a truly erotic relationship with another person.

There is no "final" analysis. The more you look at any classic fairy tale or myth or dream or work of art, the more you're liable to see.

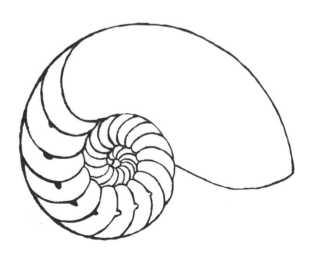

Beauty woke the next day in her father's house. A gown covered in diamonds and sewn with gold thread lay ready for her. She put it on, inwardly thanking the Beast for his kindness, and went to her father.

The merchant hugged her, and laughed, and cried for joy, all at the same time. Servants were dispatched to tell her brothers and sisters that Beauty had returned. The sisters came immediately, hoping for the worst, and were sorely disappointed to find Beauty healthy and happy, dressed like a queen, and lovelier than ever. Shortly the spiteful creatures went out into the garden, where they moaned over their sister's good fortune.

"Why should that little wretch have a gold gown?" whined one. "We're far more beautiful than she is. We must spoil her game."

"Suppose we keep her here more than a week? If we make her break her promise to the Beast, perhaps he'll finally get angry enough with her to destroy her," said the other.

When the week was up, once more the sisters rubbed their eyes with onions. They seemed so distraught and pretended such grief at the thought of her departure that Beauty agreed to stay a week more. But all the time she worried, for she knew that her longer absence would cause the Beast sorrow.

To her own surprise, she began to think tenderly of the Beast, and to miss his company in the evenings. Among all the grand and clever people who were again flocking to her father's door, she found no one who was half as sensible, or as kind.

Regarding bad impulses

Here we go again. Beauty lets herself be completely taken in by her sisters one more time. Without a firm connection to her animal nature, Beauty can't sniff out her sisters' real intentions. Because she doesn't listen to her own better judgment—her intuition—Beauty's easy to fool.

The sisters in this story are Beauty's opposite, her shadow. They stand for everything the heroine doesn't. In this case, since Beauty is all sweetness and goodness, her sisters are all meanness and evil. These girls are *bad impulses*— everything a goody-goody could not bear to admit about herself.

Bad impulses generally stay bad. If it smelled rotten last week, it's probably not gonna smell any better this week. Bad impulses don't need to be coddled, or forgiven, or treated kindly. Bad impulses don't need to be spoken sweetly to or given a second chance. Bad impulses need to be taken seriously. They need to be recognized for what they are, and dealt with immediately.

There's a good reason why the bad guys are treated so harshly in fairy tales, and one of the worst ideas in recent years was rewriting classic fairy tales to correct out the harshness. *"All three little pigs lived happily ever after and had the wolf over for tea on Thursdays"* …that is ridiculous. It's a complete misunderstanding of the way the fairy tale is supposed to function in our psyches. And furthermore, 'editing' unconscious material doesn't work any better than denial does. The more you push something from sight in one place, the more it pops up in another. The sweeter fairy tales get, the more violent video games get.

These are not real people. These are archetypes. Instinctual impulses. You have 'em, I have 'em. And some impulses deserve harsh treatment. I can't let my wicked stepmother persecute innocent people. You can't let your bloody tyrant pound someone into the ground just because he woke up on the wrong side of the bed today. These are *internal* monsters—by which I mean these babies live inside every one of our psyches—and we've all got to be tough with our internal monsters. We've got to stop them in their tracks.

When the third little pig cooks the wolf or the brothers hack Bluebeard to pieces, we are not just hearing about backward medieval violence. There's an important psychological point being made. Bad impulses don't deserve a second chance. They're dangerous. Bad impulses need to be quickly identified and firmly controlled.

It's funny how our modern world works. We're so into legislating safety for our children. And while you can control whatever you want to on the outside—strap a kid in a car seat to drive him down to the corner; make her wear a bike helmet to ride a tricycle on the sidewalk—all the laws in the world will not keep a kid from engaging in dangerous behavior when he gets older if he hasn't been taught something about controlling the violent impulses that come from *inside* his being as he grows up. The *internal* monsters are the real danger. If she can't even admit she has—much less learn how to handle—her internal monsters, she'll just get into more and more danger every year, whether she wears a bike helmet or not.

Beauty's inability to see what her shadow/sisters are up to sounds pretty much like real life. By definition, one's own shadow is hard to behold. But her vision's approaching 20-20 now when it comes to the Beast. From a distance there's room for comparison, there's time to realize what he means to her. Beauty can't appreciate some old Beast she sees every day. She has to be *deprived* of the Beast before she can see how important he is to her. And if this is a basic tendency of human nature, I fear we moderns have a bit of a problem.

Of what, dear reader, have you or I ever been deprived? Really, truly deprived? Thus, how can we possibly appreciate everything we have? Particularly when we're buried under an avalanche, a tidal wave, a tsunami, of new products every day?

There is simply no way we are ever supposed to feel satisfied with whatever we've got on hand. *"This old Beast? Egad. I really need a new one."*

Or with how *much* we've got on hand. *"Hhhhmmm… maybe I need two or three Beasts, you know, scattered here and there in a nice random pattern…"*

Or with whether or not what we've got on hand is the best thing to have on hand. *"I've been thinking… this old Beast… he's completely out of it. I want a new Beast, like that hot Italian guy I saw in People magazine yesterday."*

This other thing *would* be better, you know. It's newer. Has more functions. In fact, this other thing has so many functions you will never be able to figure out how to use them all, because you will be so busy working overtime to pay for them.

Why would it be easier for a camel to go through the eye of a needle than for a rich man to enter the gates of heaven? Because the rich man has got to be downtown picking out the new technos for the TV room in twenty minutes, dude. He ain't got time for heaven.

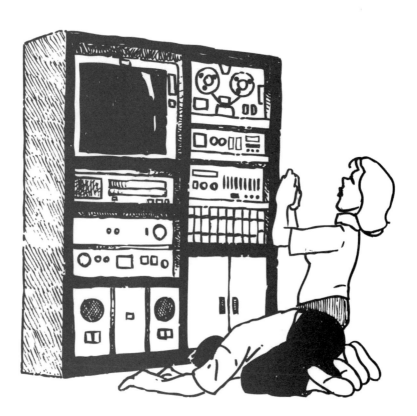

On the tenth night of her visit, Beauty dreamed she was in the garden of the palace, and that the Beast lay on the grass near the fountain, dying of despair. She jumped up immediately, regretting her long absence, and put his ring on the table.

She awoke in the castle. The hours seemed to drag as she waited impatiently for evening. At last dinnertime arrived, but still the Beast did not appear. Then Beauty, fearing he might really be dead, ran from room to room calling out for him, but there was no answer.

Remembering her dream, Beauty rushed into the garden and there at last she found the Beast, lying beside the fountain. Quite forgetting his ugliness, she bent her head to his chest and found that his heart still beat faintly, so she scooped up water from the fountain and sprinkled it on his face.

The Beast opened his eyes. " I couldn't live without you, Beauty. But I'll die happily now that I've seen you again."

" No, dear Beast!" cried Beauty. " Don't die. I love you. Live, Beast! Live! Be my husband, and allow me to be your wife."

At Beauty's words the castle burst into light. Fireworks and music filled the air. The Beast disappeared, and in his place stood a handsome Prince.

" But where's my Beast?" sobbed Beauty.

" I'm your Beast," replied the Prince. " I was enchanted and changed into a monstrous beast, forbidden to show I had sense or wit until someone should love me for myself alone. You judged me by my heart, Beauty. Take it then, and all that I have besides, for all is yours."

Then the Prince led Beauty inside the castle, where she found all her family, brought there by the beautiful lady from her dream.

" Beauty," said the fairy, " you've chosen well, and now you'll be rewarded. You shall be a great queen."

Then the fairy turned to Beauty's sisters. " Your punishment will be to see your sister's happiness. From this moment on you'll be stone statues at the door of your sister's palace, and you'll stay that way until you realize your envious natures, which I fear may be a long time indeed."

Then the fairy transported them all to the Prince's true kingdom, where his people received them with great joy.

There he and Beauty were married, became king and queen, ruled well, and lived happily ever after.

Happily ever after

There you have it. Beauty did not get rid of her Beast by denying him, or by fighting him, or by blaming his actions on someone else, or by calling him the devil. She got rid of her Beast by claiming him. As her own. She willingly and lovingly took that old Beast into her heart, which allowed him to become human again, to reenter the daylight world. And not just any old human being, either—an exceptional human being: a prince and a king.

Bly says: "Most of the juice is in the shadow."[y] Meaning: our most vital, creative and powerful energies are usually trapped underneath our daytime personalities while we try to "fit in" and appear "normal." If we consciously—with intent, by thinking about it—pull out part of that submerged energy and start working with it, our lives will be immeasurably enriched. In this story, when Beauty married her 'higher' thoughts to her 'lower' feelings, she became a "great queen."

Dreams are one way to work with part of that submerged energy. They provide a direct connection between instinct and intellect, between unconscious and conscious processes. An honest attempt to understand the symbols in your dreams and to adjust your outer reality to your inner vision will go a long way toward marrying your Beauty to your Beast.

For one thing, in our dreams we can say things to ourselves we wouldn't let anyone else say to us. It's a lot easier to take advice from your own psyche than it is to take advice from other people. For another thing, we come straight from the factory equipped with parts far older and more experienced than our thinking minds. When operating any vehicle, it just seems silly not to use all the equipment provided. See the "Recommended Books" list for information about working with dreams. A good place to start is *Every Dreamer's Handbook*, by Will Phillips.[z]

You can also reach "down" into your unconscious through a physical

medium, by doing something that lets your hands and
your body express what's going on in your soul: *Writing
Drawing Painting Dancing Storytelling Singing
Sculpting Sewing Gardening Building Playing
Music...*

Civilization forces its components to specialize.
Like machine parts, we do one type of thing, over and
over again, day after day. What's worse, we've gotten to
where we describe ourselves as only one type of thing.
"I'm an engineer." Thus we've gotten to the point where
we think only "artists" have enough talent to produce
works of imagination. That's soul depriving. Especially since we're not talking
about talent, anyway. Talent is not required for shadow work. We're talking
about creativity, about using the light of imagination to explore the dark places
in the soul; about being creative for no gain whatsoever except spiritual. About
using some of that crazy energy you usually try to pretend you don't have,
without hurting anybody else.

Listening to yourself is another surefire method for uncovering shadow
material. What makes you mutter under your breath? Who do you just *hate?*
That emotional intensity comes directly from your shadow. You wouldn't care all
that much if it didn't have something to do with a sorely neglected part of your
own psyche.

Blaming how you feel on someone else will not make the feeling any easier
to bear. Admitting that it's your feeling (being honest about where it comes
from), seeing what you need to do about it (dealing responsibly with it), and
expressing it creatively through some sort of body/mind activity
(rather than merely projecting it onto others) *will* make it easier
to bear.

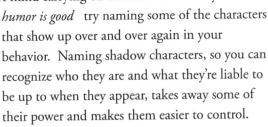

If you don't mind carrying on conversations with yourself
humor is good try naming some of the characters
that show up over and over again in your
behavior. Naming shadow characters, so you can
recognize who they are and what they're liable to
be up to when they appear, takes away some of
their power and makes them easier to control.

Two of my recurring characters are **The
Preacher** *{Surprise!}* and **The Princess**. **The
Preacher** always thinks he knows what other
people ought to be doing, and goes on missions
to tell them so. I have to knock him off his

soapbox occasionally by pointing out that he doesn't know shit about other people's situations and is simply avoiding his own issues. **The Princess** simply cannot *believe* she has so many grubby menial jobs. Where on *earth* are her servants? Her gardener, her maid, her cook? This dame can get in a real snit about performing simple household chores. But statistics usually work on her. I point out how many people in the world don't have homes at all, much less chores, and ask her how she'd like to be not just busy, but homeless.

What's interesting is how much value both **The Preacher** and **The Princess** add to my personality as long as I don't let them get out of hand. **The Preacher** cares about soul, about making the world a better place. Without the old goat's continual nagging and prodding I would have never finished this book. **The Princess** expects grace and order. She has a good eye, and likes to throw parties. Without her infernal fussy standards my home would still be a shack in the woods and my garden would be overrun with weeds. I *need* both characters in my psyche. I just don't need to let them drive me—or anybody else—crazy.

What kind of characters show up over and over again in your behavior? Got a **Whiner** in there? How about a **Bully**, or a **Clown**? Or maybe that perennial favorite: **A Helpless Victim of Bad Parenting**. Whoever they are, name them. *Name the characters you play.* Find out what they want, and why they keep showing up—how they hurt you and how they help you. *Invite them out into the light of consciousness.* But don't let any one of them get away with thinking they run the whole show, with thinking that they're *you*.

Unconscious forces are amoral—not concerned with right or wrong, just concerned with getting their own way; instinctual results of evolution, nature and nurture. If we really want to be considered "higher beings," then we have an ethical responsibility to examine our unconscious urges whenever possible and try to bring them into line with our conscious stances—to honor those old archetypal presences with our feelings, but to temper their expression with our moral intelligence.

At birth we're a part of everything. As we grow older we learn to discriminate, to practice that which seems to work in our culture and to hide that which doesn't. If we ever grow up—a lonely process in a culture which values youth more than wisdom—we do so by going back and looking for the parts of our souls that we hid from others in order to fit in. In other words, if we ever mature, we do so by thinking about what we've stuffed into our shadows. This process closes the circle of life. It makes a ring.

The ring is one of humanity's oldest, most sacred symbols. It stands for totality. Enclosure. The uroboros (a serpent with his own tail in his mouth) appears on extremely ancient shards of pottery, signifying the universal womb encircling all of life. Romans proudly displayed the disc of *Sol Invictus*, the halo graces Christian artwork, the mandala is essential to Eastern meditation, and the sand paintings of the Navaho are circular, as were the tepees spread across the Plains.

Rings hold things, rings connect things, rings appear at openings—think of jars and bottles and baskets and mouths of caves. The very planet we live on is a circle, traveling ceaselessly in a ring around the sun. Rings symbolically express the soul's deepest desire: to reconnect, to reach a state of totality, to become whole.[aa] So when Beauty wanted to return to the Beast, she had to put his ring on the table.

Putting the ring on the table is not about perfecting whatever masks you've learned to wear for your family and your friends. It's about looking underneath those masks. It's about marrying your cultured Beauty to your archetypal Beast. It's about getting those old animal instincts and that shiny new human intellect to cooperate with one another and enrich one another and police one another.

Wow. Now that would be amazing. Wonder if it's ever been done… well of course it's been done. Those are the people who move humanity forward—the *ring* leaders. And they're also ordinary people like you and me who follow their own hearts. Rosa Parks comes to mind here. She simply sat down and wouldn't budge, no matter what. Changed her whole country for the better.

The water of the fountain is another splendid symbol. For a human being on the planet Earth, water is the difference between a garden and a desert, between living and dying. Second in importance only to breath, water is one of the things we absolutely have to have, thus it symbolizes spiritual as well as physical nourishment—the Fountain of Life. When Beauty sprinkles the Beast with water she brings him back to life. He's being baptized, reborn, into the human realm.

Now the Beast, that old predominantly feminine, instinctual, animal nature who was relegated to the dark and stormy forests of the unconscious at the beginning of this story, may live openly in Beauty's new masculine world of civilized, linear, rational thinking. Now the shadowy character can step out into the light. And when he does so with the *cooperation of consciousness*, his beastly nature is transformed into a princely nature. **"Married" together, the Beast and the Beauty, the old animal**

instincts and the new human practice of rational thinking, form a perfect union.

And what happens to those bad grrlz, the shrew sisters? The fairy lets them have it. Turns them into stone without a moment's hesitation. Alas, this does not mean we can pour concrete shoes for anyone who ticks us off. It means we're supposed to deal firmly with bad impulses, whether they're coming from within (our own hearts), or from without (the world around us). Stone—firmly.

Notice the fairy doesn't get rid of the sisters. That's because she can't. It simply isn't possible. As Ursula K. LeGuin said in *The Left Hand of Darkness,*

> Light is the left hand of darkness,
> Darkness the right hand of light.[ab]

The two opposites fit together to make a whole. And since the collective unconscious stretching back behind us for thousands of years contains just as many ogres as wise men, there's no way any human being is ever going to be free from flaws. Bad impulses are here to stay. **Bad impulses are as much a part of our common humanity as good impulses.**

However, the beautiful fairy does give us a way forward. Her solution is to clearly identify the bad impulses and keep them under control. She puts the shadow sisters right out front by the gates, and **that just might be the highest form of personal wisdom: putting your shadow right out front where you can keep an eye on it; admitting your bad points whenever you can, and then working to keep them under control.** It certainly sounds more workable for humanity in the long run than merely denying your bad points and projecting them onto others. *{Less hatred.}*

If accepting responsibility for shadow material is the highest form of personal wisdom, then **the highest form of collective wisdom would be demanding that our leaders and our countries do the same. No more doublethink, no more newspeak, no more covert actions—but true diplomacy, practiced out in the open, among**

respected equals. Whatever happened to the Golden Rule? Have corporate interests made it obsolete? If it's not business a country can be proud of doing right out front by the gates, if it's not business a country wouldn't want done to it, then the country shouldn't be doing the business. *{Less exploitation. Less warfare.}*

The "Prince's true kingdom" is the soul. "Ruling well" in this interior kingdom requires a marriage—a true union—of masculine qualities and feminine qualities, of intellectual prowess and intuitive feeling, of ancient ways and modern techniques, of civilized manners and savage energy. Unions of opposites, not dueling dualities.

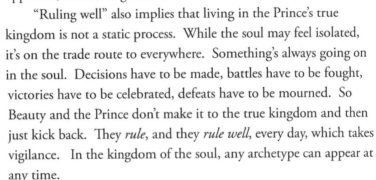

"Ruling well" also implies that living in the Prince's true kingdom is not a static process. While the soul may feel isolated, it's on the trade route to everywhere. Something's always going on in the soul. Decisions have to be made, battles have to be fought, victories have to be celebrated, defeats have to be mourned. So Beauty and the Prince don't make it to the true kingdom and then just kick back. They *rule*, and they *rule well*, every day, which takes vigilance. In the kingdom of the soul, any archetype can appear at any time.

Any archetype can appear at any time… now that's downright frightening. There are some pretty grotesque characters prowling around in every human psyche. Knowing that, accepting that, is the first step toward ruling well. You cannot control a behavior if you cannot even admit you might be capable of practicing it.

However, 'any archetype can appear at any time' also means there are some pretty wonderful characters prowling around in every human psyche. Like the dare to be different, one of a kind thinkers and creators. Like the gods and goddesses, the heroes and heroines. Like the handsome prince and the beautiful lady in the dream.

What might ordinary citizens of the Prince's true kingdom be like? Probably people who have let go of perfect and are just trying to stay in balance—a process which changes with every step. And I bet they have dream clubs, the way we have book clubs, where they get together and pore over the symbols in their dreams.

But, no doubt about it, I *know* people in the Prince's true kingdom would go outside occasionally. Surely they wouldn't be dumb enough to spend all their time indoors, like the woman writing this book right now.

...and

HAPPILY EVER AFTER...
ah, who knows?

Perhaps happily ever after can only

be found inside fleeting moments

on uncharted islands

in the Sea of the Soul ...

Endnotes

a   Clarissa Pinkola Estes, *Women Who Run With the Wolves*. New York: Ballantine Books, 1992. 16-17.

b   James Hillman and Michael Ventura, *We've Had 100 Years of Psychotherapy and the World's Getting Worse*. SanFrancisco: Harper, 1992.

c   Thomas Moore, *Care of the Soul*. New York: HarperPerennial, 1994. 18-20.

d   Joseph Campbell, *Hero With A Thousand Faces*. Bollingen Series XVII, Princeton: Princeton University Press, 1973.

e   Robert Bly, "The Human Shadow," Lecture at Open Center, New York City. Recorded and edited by William Booth, Audiotape, Sound Horizons, 1991. Parts of this lecture are included in *A Little Book on the Human Shadow*, also written by Robert Bly and edited by William Booth. San Francisco: Harper, 1988.

f   Joseph Campbell with Bill Moyers, *The Power of Myth*. New York: Doubleday Anchor Books, 1998. 167-173.

g   Joseph Campbell, *Occidental Mythology: The Masks of God, Volume III*. New York: Penguin Books, 1976.

h   Erich Neumann, *The Origins and History of Consciousness*. Bollingen Series XLII, Princeton: Princeton University Press, 1973. 288.

i   Riane Eisler, *The Chalice and the Blade; Our History, Our Future*. HarperSanFrancisco, 1987.

j   Neumann, 158-161.

k   Jeanne-Marie Leprince de Beaumont, *"Beauty and the Beast," The Fairy Tale Book*. Translated by Marie Ponsot, illustrated by Adrienne Segur. New York: Golden Press, 1958. 96-101.

l   C. G. Jung, *The Portable Jung*, Edited by Joseph Campbell. New York: Penguin Books, 1971. 145.

m   Bly, 1991. Bly actually said, "witch." But I just can't go there, so I substituted "bad actors."

n   Ibid.

o   C.G. Jung, source unknown. Here's an example of my village idiot: this is one of the first things I ran into when I began researching the human shadow, one of the quotes that inspired my quest. But about five years ago, in a fit of "I am not writing a book on the human shadow and that's that," I put several folders full of notes into the recycling bin, thus the correct reference to this quote disappeared. I think it's from the foreward to the 1954 hardback edition of *Depth Psychology And A New Ethic*, by Erich Neumann, but I can only find later paperback editions now, with a different foreward. If you know the correct reference, please let me know. It's a great quote.

p   Howard Zinn, *A People's History of the United States*. New York: HarperCollins, 2003. 421-25.

q   Paul Simon, "Graceland." Audio CD, Warner Bros., 1997. (Enhanced re-release.)

r   C. G. Jung, editor, *Man and His Symbols*. New York: Doubleday Anchor Books, 1964.

s   George Orwell, *1984*. New York: Harcourt, Brace and Company, Inc., 1949.

t   Zinn, 2003.

u   John Perkins, *Confessions of an Economic Hit Man*. San Francisco: Berret-Koehler Publishers, 2004.

v   Stephen Kinzer, *Overthrow, America's Century of Regime Change from Hawaii to Iraq*. New York: Times Books, Henry Holt and Company, 2006.

w   Ibid, 23.

x   Robert Louis Stevenson, *"The Strange Case of Dr. Jekyll and Mr. Hyde,"* in Master's Library: Robert Louis Stevenson. London: Octopus Books Limited, 1984.

y   Bly, 1991.

z   Will Phillips, *Every Dreamers Handbook*. New York: Kensington Books, 1994.

aa   C. G. Jung, *The Portable Jung*, 324.

ab   Ursula K. LeGuin, *"The Left Hand of Darkness,"* in Ursula K. LeGuin: Five Complete Novels. New York: Avenvel Books, 1985. 450.

Recommended Books

The Human Shadow

A Little Book on the Human Shadow, Robert Bly. HarperSanFrancisco, 1988. This "little" book contains a huge amount of life-changing information.

The Human Shadow, Robert Bly. Audiocassettes of a live lecture, edited by William Booth, Sound Horizons, 1991. This is a lecture given at the Open Center in New York on the subjects covered in that "little" book above, and it is without a doubt the single best work ever done by any one individual on the human shadow. It's dated now—he's referring to George Sr., not George Jr.— but it's powerful. Bly uses poetry, story, music and compassion for his audience to talk kindly yet forcefully about the human shadow. If you can listen to this whole lecture without feeling uneasy about something, you're dead already. Perhaps if enough of us ask for it Sound Horizons will update and re-release this lecture on CD.

Evil, The Shadow Side of Reality, John Sanford. Crossroad Publishing, New York, 1994. Don't let the title scare you off. This is a very good book. Sanford is an Episcopalian priest as well as a well-known Jungian psychologist and author, so he's examining the ever present problem of evil from several perspectives: psychological, Christian, philosophical, mythological and literary.

Meeting the Shadow, The Hidden Power of the Dark Side of Human Nature, Edited by Connie Zweig & Jeremiah Abrams. Jeremy P. Tarcher, Inc., 1991. This is a treasure chest of information about the human shadow—it contains 65 different essays on the human shadow by everyone from Sam Keen to Scott Peck. Highly recommended.

Owning Your Own Shadow, Understanding the Dark Side of the Psyche, Robert A. Johnson. HarperSanFrancisco, 1991. Johnson is a Jungian analyst and the author of *Inner Work*, listed below in Dreamwork. Here he emphasizes the necessity of looking beyond opposites, the importance of consciously honoring the shadow, and the value of embracing paradox.

People of the Lie, the Hope for Curing Human Evil, M. Scott Peck. Touchstone, 1985. In this book Peck examines what often lies underneath the "nice" in what we refer to as a "nice" person. It's well worth examining. As Jung said once, "I'd rather be whole than good."

Romancing the Shadow, A Guide to Soul Work for a Vital, Authentic Life, Connie Zweig & Steve Wolf. Ballantine Wellspring, 1999. Paperback; *(or)*

Romancing the Shadow, Illuminating the Dark Side of the Soul, Connie Zweig & Steve Wolf, Ballantine Books, 1997. Hardcover. The "introduction to shadow-work" in these books is thorough and informative, as is the authors' explanation of the difference between the over-medicated medical model of psychology and the more introspective Jungian approach. Then they delve into numerous case histories illustrating how the human shadow effects life and relationships. Easy to read and extremely helpful.

Shadow and Evil in Fairy Tales*,* Marie-Louise von Franz. Spring Publications, 1974. As a student and close friend of Jung's, von Franz has a unique historical perspective. Plus, her writing is warm-hearted, direct and uncluttered. This book examines how the shadow manifests in civilizations through fairy tales. More books by von Franz below in Jungian Thought.

SHADOW Searching for the Hidden Self, Archetypes of the Collective Unconscious,
Vol. 1, Anthology*,* Tarcher/Putnam, 2002. This gorgeous book has an introduction by Robert Bly and 24 different stories by authors like Stephen King, Joyce Carol Oates, Anne Sexton, Edgar Allen Poe, and Nathaniel Hawthorne. Plus, it's illustrated on practically every page with full-color-artwork by modern American artists. A beautiful, chilling glimpse into the shadow of America through literature and art.

Why Good People Do Bad Things: Understanding Our Darker Selves, James Hollis. Gotham Books, Penguin Group, 2007. Alas, our good intentions are often thwarted by our bad attitudes. And Hollis is brave enough to look at how unrecognized shadow material affects us culturally as well as personally. Our search for the "Other" as he calls it, for someone who'll take care of us—or someone we can blame—ultimately leads us right back to ourselves.

Politics, Culture, History

An Inconvenient Truth: The Planetary Emergency of Global Warming and What We Can Do About It*,* Al Gore. Rodale Press, 2006. Global warming shares quite a few qualities with the human shadow—extremely inconvenient, highly uncomfortable to acknowledge, hard to start working on, usually denied. Al Gore is a true hero; a man who keeps on going to bat for what he believes in no matter how heartbreaking his last strike out. An academy award-winning documentary of *An Inconvenient Truth* is also available on DVD.

A People's History of the United States, 1492-Present*,* Howard Zinn. HarperCollins, 2003. When you first see the size of this book you think you won't be able to finish it. Then when you start reading it, you won't be able to put it down. It should be required reading for every citizen of the USA. What we aren't told, compared to what we are told, is simply astonishing. And Zinn is fearless—he never pulls his punches.

The Assault on Reason, Al Gore. Penguin Press, 2007. Not running for office sure frees a guy up to speak his mind. This book kicks some serious ass. "When the public merely watches and listens and does not have a speaking part, the entire exercise is fraudulent. It might be called *American Democracy: The Movie*. It looks and sounds almost real, but its true purpose is the presentation of a semblance of participatory democracy in order to produce a counterfeit version of the consent of the governed."

The Chalice and the Blade, Our History, Our Future, Riane Eisler. HarperSanFrancisco, 1987. A review of the mounting archaeological evidence which suggests that human beings did not always live in patriarchal, warlike societies, and do not necessarily have to in the future. Now that's good news.

Collapse, How Societies Choose to Fail or Succeed, Jared Diamond. Penguin Group, 2005. Diamond (author of *Guns, Germs and Steel*) has done us a big favor here. He makes it clear that whether we ultimately fail or succeed as a society is entirely up to us, examines the choices made by present and past societies which led to their success or failure, and offers suggestions for the future.

Confessions of An Economic Hit Man, John Perkins. Berrett-Koehler, 2004. A chilling book. Why do rock stars keep trying to get Third-World loans cancelled? Turns out most of the loans are bogus—merely fronts for big business interests. The smooth talking representatives go over and say "You guys need a dam (or a bridge or whatever). Let us build one for you!" Then the countries go deeply into debt to a giant corporation for something they really didn't need which completely destroys their way of life and leaves them too broke to provide basic services for their own people. In most cases the money never leaves the USA.

Fast Food Nation, The Dark Side of the American Meal, Eric Schlosser. HarperCollins, 2002. I think that title says it all.

Fiasco: The American Military Misadventure in Iraq, Thomas E. Ricks. Penguin Press, 2007. I hate to recommend such a sad book, but we should all read it anyway. If our current fiasco in Iraq does indeed lead to the decline of the American empire, at least we'll all know what happened. Written by a Senior Pentagon Correspondent for the Washington Post.

The Future of Success, Working and Living in the New Economy, Robert B. Reich. Vintage Books/Random House, 2000. A former Secretary of Labor and a very bright man with a very big heart, Reich is always worth a look. In this book he makes telling points about what's awry in our time, without letting any of us off the hook about how things got that way. I was particularly struck by what he calls "sorting:" the way we all unconsciously sort ourselves into communities and neighborhoods and school districts to the exclusion of those who have less resources than we do, and the impact it will have on our culture if not mitigated by other factors..

Overthrow, America's Century of Regime Change from Hawaii to Iraq, Stephen Kinzer. Times Books, Henry Holt & Co., 2006. Absolute proof that the USA's heroic rhetoric does not always match her clandestine actions. Meticulously documented evidence of the *14 governments toppled by the USA* since 1893. Ouch.

The Sibling Society, Robert Bly. Addison-Wesley, 1996. Bly points out that the USA has become a nation of squabbling siblings because no one is willing to grow up. We refuse to take up the mantle of "elder" no matter how old we get, and we neglect the acquisition of wisdom to buy increasingly elaborate toys and manipulate our bodies to look young. A good book for aging baby boomers in denial about what awaits us around the next bend.

The United States of Europe, The New Superpower and the End of American Supremacy, T.R. Reid. Penguin Press, 2004. Reid spent months living in Europe, and comes out with a much different perspective than we get from this side of the globe. Cooperation between countries, although far from easy or painless, has led to phenomenal progress in Europe—a lesson for the USA in not always getting your own way.

 # Mythology, Comparative Religion

The Battle for God, A History of Fundamentalism, Karen Armstrong. Ballantine/Random House, 2000. Twentieth-century fundamentalism "is a reaction against the scientific and secular culture that first appeared in the West, but which has since taken root in other parts of the world." And the reason to study it? "It is no good pretending that the fundamentalist threat does not exist, or dismissing fundamentalism with secularist disdain as the preoccupation of a few deluded crazy people. History shows that attempts to suppress fundamentalism simply make it more extreme."

See ***The Chalice and the Blade,*** in Politics, Culture & History, above.

The Flight of the Wild Gander, Explorations in the Mythological Dimensions of Fairy Tales, Legends and Symbols, Joseph Campbell. HarperPerennial, 1990. One of Campbell's most accessible books, which contains extremely useful descriptions of what happens to reality if one insists on taking religious metaphors as historical facts. (For instance, if the actual, physical body of Jesus started to ascend toward "heaven" 2000 years ago, even if it went at the speed of light, which is not possible for a physical body, he would still not be out of our galaxy.) The title refers to the wild ganders that often figured as totem spirits for Shamans in Northern tribes and as symbols of enlightenment in India. Campbell, like Neumann below, felt that at this point in human evolution each person has to become their own shaman, has to learn to follow the flight of their own wild gander, in order to soar.

The Golden Ass, Apuleius. Translated by Robert Graves, Farrar, Straus & Giroux, 1979. Written in the second century CE, this is one of the funniest, bawdiest books you will ever read. It also contains the most famous version of one of the oldest animal husband stories, *Cupid and Psyche.*

The Great Mother, Erich Neumann, translated by Ralph Manheim. Bollingen Series, Princeton, 1991. The archetype whose influence—for good and for evil—none of us can escape, described in detail as it appears from the earliest dawn of human culture down to the present time, with hundreds of pictures of artwork from all over the world. If you get bored with Neumann's pedantry, you can just look at the pictures.

The Great Transformation, The Beginning of Our Religious Traditions, Karen Armstrong. Anchor Books, Random House, 2006. From about 900 to 200 BCE (what German philosopher Carl Jaspers called the "Axial Age"), four traditions that continue to shape world thought were born: monotheism in Israel, Confucianism and Daoism in China, Hinduism and Buddhism in India, and philosophical rationalism in Greece. Armstrong beautifully and thoroughly describes each of these developments, and makes it clear that only a return to the core insight of all four traditions—treat others as you wish to be treated—can provide a way forward for humanity.

The Greek Myths, Robert Graves. Penguin Books, 1996. Introduction by Kenneth McLeish, illustrations by Grahame Baker. This is a beautifully illustrated hard cover edition of Graves' 1955 classic. Everything you ever wanted to—OK, OK, more than you ever wanted to—know about Greek myths, with Graves' analysis after each major grouping. Whether or not you always agree with his conclusions, it's a valuable reference and a fascinating read.

The Hero With A Thousand Faces, Joseph Campbell. Bollingen Series, Princeton, 1973. An absolute classic. The book that put Joseph Campbell on the map. I will always remember when my son, who was in high school at the time, looked up from reading this book to say, "Wow. This is awesome! Joseph Campbell must've studied for years to put all this together, and now all I hafta do is read this one book!" Exactly.

A History of God, The 4,000-Year Quest of Judaism, Christianity, and Islam, Karen Armstrong. Ballantine/Random House, 1993. This is a history of monotheism, from Babylon to the present—how these religions came into being, and how they influenced and shaped one another. It's an eminently readable book absolutely crammed with well-documented historical information. Now that's hard to do.

The Masks of God: Volume I, Primitive Mythology; Volume II, Oriental Mythology; Volume III, Occidental Mythology; Volume IV, Creative Mythology; Joseph Campbell. Penguin Books, 1976. I have to put these books in here, because they're incredibly important to me. I also have to warn you that it took me a year—yes, that's right, one whole year—to read and study them to my own satisfaction. In other words, these books are not casual reading. Campbell was a spiritual historian, and in these books he's giving us the whole spiritual history of humanity as accurately as it could be given at the time he wrote the books. They're difficult, and they refer to about 50 other books that you'll have to read to keep up, but they're absolutely worth the effort for anyone curious about the history and the future of the human spirit.

Myths to Live By, Joseph Campbell. Penguin Compass, 1972. This book contains 12 essays derived from 25 different lectures originally given at the Cooper Union Forum in New York. The results are inspiring, informative comparisons of the world's major religions. What's the difference between Mahayana Buddhism and Zen Buddhism? Why do so many world myths feature virgin births? What are those chakra things? etc. Find out by reading this book.

The Origins and History of Consciousness, Erich Neumann. Bollingen Series, Princeton University Press, 1954. This is a dated book and difficult to read, but it has an interesting and well-developed premise: that myths and religions evolved the way they did in response to humanity's emerging consciousness, which is still emerging.

The Power of Myth, Joseph Campbell with Bill Moyers, Edited by Betty Sue Flowers. Doubleday, 1988. If you only get one book by Joseph Campbell, this should be it. (No! *Reflections on the Art of Living!* No! *Myths To Live By!* Oh, shoot. Just get several.) And make sure you get the illustrated edition of this one. It contains the entire, now famous dialogue between Bill Moyers and Joseph Campbell that regularly appears on public television at fund-raising time. Moyers' questions slow Campbell's brain down enough for the rest of us to keep up, and the stunning illustrations on every page make it a visual delight.

Reflections on the Art of Living, A Joseph Campbell Companion, Selected and edited by Diane K. Osbon. HarperPerennial, 1991. My absolute favorite. A book to open at random anytime you need comfort or inspiration, compiled from excerpts of a month-long seminar JC taught at Esalen Institute. "Every moment is utterly unique and will not be continued in eternity. This fact gives life its poignancy and should concentrate your attention on what you are experiencing now. I think that's washed out a bit by the notion that everyone will be happy later in heaven. You had better be happy here, now. You'd better experience the eternal here and now."

Dreamwork

Diamonds of the Night, The Search for Spirit in Your Dreams, James Hagan. PageMill Press, 1997. As the author says in the introduction, "This is a book for ordinary people, people who do not have a doctorate degree, but who will read and understand. For that reason, the book has been written in plain language, with brevity, without footnotes, and with as little scientific language as possible." A valuable book for anyone interested in doing dream work.

Every Dreamer's Handbook, A Step-by-step Guide to Understanding and Benefiting from your Dreams, Will Phillips. Kensington Books, 1994. Phillips takes the mystery and anxiety out of studying your own dreams, bless his heart. Simple enough for a twelve year old, effective enough for anybody.

Healing Dreams, Marc Ian Barasch. Riverhead Books, New York, 2000. The author has collected dream experiences from all sorts of cultures, from all over the world. He primarily focuses on "big dreams," the ones that change your life if you heed them, but there's also a helpful section on how our shadows affect our dreams. Interesting reading, thought provoking material.

Inner Work, Using Dreams and Active Imagination for Personal Growth, Robert Johnson. HarperSan Francisco, 1986. Johnson offers an accessible, four-step approach to dream work that he developed during his practice as a Jungian analyst, and maintains that people can do dream work on their own by proceeding consciously and carefully through these steps. For the truly courageous, he also offers a four-step procedure for practicing active imagination, with appropriate warnings.

New Directions in Dream Interpretation, Edited by Gayle Delaney. State University of New York Press, 1993. Seven modern approaches to dream interpretation described by the practicing psychologists and psychiatrists who use them. Written for the profession, but also readable for us lay folk.

Where People Fly and Water Runs Uphill, Using Dreams to Tap the Wisdom of the Unconscious, Jeremy Taylor. Warner Books, 1992. Taylor is a co-founder of the Association for the Study of Dreams. This book includes techniques for working with groups, for improving dream recall, for working by oneself, and a list of recommended books for further study.

Jungian Thought

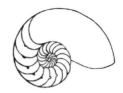

Archetypal Dimensions of the Psyche, Marie-Louise von Franz. Shambhala, 1999. The human race is in transition—rigid old cultural and religious rules no longer apply to our lives; new ways of living in contact with our bodies and with nature, new ethical standards, will be required. Here von Franz presents mythological examples of how the collective psyche points toward, and can guide us through, this transition period.

Archetypal Patterns in Fairy Tales, Marie-Louise von Franz. Inner City Books, 1997. In-depth interpretations of six fairy tales from six different countries. Another good book from von Franz. See The Interpretation of Fairy Tales, below.

Care of the Soul, A Guide for Cultivating Depth and Sacredness in Everyday Life, Thomas Moore. HarperPerennial, 1992. Moore advocates learning to care for yourself, rather than trying to cure yourself. Simple and powerful advice. Also see *Soul Mates*, by Moore, listed below.

The Interpretation of Fairy Tales, Marie-Louise von Franz. Shambhala, 1996. Jungians analyze classic fairy tales because they're one of the simplest and purest expressions of the collective unconscious, and as such they offer rich glimpses into basic patterns of human behavior. In this book von Franz describes the steps involved in analyzing a fairy tale, and then uses these steps to discuss a variety of European tales.

Iron John, A Book About Men, Robert Bly. Addison-Wesley, 1990. A ground-breaking work about male initiation, the role of the mentor in a man's life, and the reality of being male as opposed to the stereotype of being male that permeates modern life. Highly recommended for both men and women.

The Maiden King, The Reunion of Masculine and Feminine, Robert Bly and Marion Woodman. Henry Holt and Company, 1998. Woodman, a Jungian analyst, joins Bly here and together the two, male and female, examine the same story to illustrate how far removed masculine and feminine principles have become from one another in modern life and to suggest steps which could be taken to bring them back together in the future.

Man and His Symbols, Edited by Carl Jung. Doubleday Anchor Books, 1964. An old book and a gorgeous book. The numerous illustrations from art, film, and life on every page make the role that symbols play in our psyches graphically clear. Definitely the easiest of Jung's books to read, and an interesting book historically too, as most of his life Jung refused to write for the general public, fearing it would only lead to misunderstanding. Then he dreamed in his waning years that he should try to reach the masses and this book—a collaboration between Jung and some of his closest colleagues—was the result. Get the hardback with all the artwork. It's a collectible item.

Memories, Dreams, Reflections, C.G. Jung, recorded and edited by Aniela Jaffe, translated by Richard and Clara Winston. Vintage Books Edition, 1989. If there is any spark of the visionary, the artist, the impossible dreamer, or the heroic introvert in your soul, you need to read this book. Spoken aloud to Jaffe and/or hand-written in the last 4 years of his life, this is a candid glimpse into the psyche of a truly unique individual—a man who really did follow his own heart.

Men and the Water of Life, Michael Meade. HarperSanFrancisco, 1993. This is simply a great book, in any genre. I took it on a road trip once and read passages aloud to my whole family, who were enthralled. When telling a story, Meade can get more mileage out of a metaphor than any person on earth, and when recounting his real-life experiences as a conscientious objector to the Vietnam war—including prison—Meade is mesmerizing.

The Myth of Analysis, Three Essays in Archetypal Psychology, James Hillman. Northwestern University Press, 1972. James Hillman has written a slew of books and has profoundly influenced the entire post-Jungian psychological community. He's a courageous, original thinker. I love the hell out of him. I have a shelf full of his books. But this is the only book of his that I'm putting on this list because it's the only one that doesn't make me grind my teeth at some point while reading it. Hillman has terrific ideas, but he tends to take off with those ideas into the stratosphere. I recommend him for practiced, critical readers who will sift through his ideas and form their own opinions as they read.

The Portable Jung, Edited by Joseph Campbell. Penguin Books, 1971. This is the most dog-eared, highlighted, written in, and worn out edition of Jung's work at my house. Written by Jung, and edited by Campbell—each man a visionary and a genius.

Soul Mates, Honoring the Mysteries of Love and Relationship, Thomas Moore. HarperCollins, 1994. Here Moore applies the idea he explored in *Care of the Soul*—"caring for" rather than "curing"—to how couples relate to one another. Very useful.

Women Who Run With the Wolves, Myths and Stories of the Wild Woman Archetype, Clarissa Pinkola Estes. Ballantine Books, 1992. A terrific book. Estes is a Jungian analyst, a great story teller, and a loving heart. Her passion for life is infectious, her courage to look life right in the face inspiring. Highly recommended for both men and women.

Literature

Authors who aren't afraid to show a little shadow in their work:

Sherman Alexie	Ursula K. LeGuin
Margaret Atwood	D.H. Lawrence
Joseph Conrad	Herman Melville
Fyodor Dostoyevsky	Joyce Carol Oates
Dave Eggers	Flannery O'Connor
Louise Erdrich	Edgar Allan Poe
William Faulkner	Toni Morrison
Nadine Gordimer	Annie Proulx
Nathaniel Hawthorne	Wallace Stegner
Franz Kafka	John Trudell
Stephen King	Alice Walker
Barbara Kingsolver	Edith Wharton

GRR...

...and Specifics

1984, George Orwell. For $2.95—thousands of used copies exist on the Internet—you can have one of the best books ever written. How Orwell knew in 1949 what many places in the world would look like today is one of the great artistic mysteries. And the mid-book explanation of 'why there must always be a war' is worth any price. You cannot pretend to be educated until you've read this book. There's a film version of *1984* starring Richard Burton as the bad guy.

Always Coming Home, Ursula K. LeGuin. Harper & Row, 1985. First off, LeGuin is my hero. She's written close to 40 critically acclaimed books while raising a family. And versatile doesn't begin to describe her work: novels, short stories, science fiction, criticism, poetry, children's books. The common thread in them all is the way LeGuin bravely explores the innermost reaches of what it means to be human—this woman writes *soul* fiction. *The Left Hand of Darkness, Four Ways to Forgiveness, The Dispossessed, The Lathe of Heaven, Searoad, The Wizard of Earthsea* series (listed below). This particular book, *Always Coming Home*, is a Utopian novel that takes place in Northern California several thousand years after an apocalyptic meltdown on the planet Earth. Appropriately, it's written in experimental form. You can read it straight through, or you can skip around. Either way, when you've finished the book your only question will be, "How do we get to Kesh?"

The Da Vinci Code, Dan Brown. Doubleday, 2003. And why not? A rip roaring mystery that re-introduces symbology, teaches quite a bit of history, and poses some interesting questions.

The Rag and Bone Shop of the Heart, Poems for Men, Anthology, edited by Robert Bly, James Hillman and Michael Meade. HarperCollins, 1993. Poetry by men and about men collected from all over the world by three renowned author/ titans of the men's movement. Poignant, powerful, heartbreaking, inspiring… just about everything you need.

SHADOW Searching for the Hidden Self, Archetypes of the Collective Unconscious, Vol 1
Described in the first section above.

The Strange Case of Dr. Jekyll and Mr. Hyde, Robert Louis Stevenson. Another instance where you can have a great book for pennies by looking on the Internet. There are also several film versions of *Dr. Jekyll & Mr. Hyde*. The truest to the spirit of the book is the version starring Fredric March.

The Wizard of Earthsea, series of six books: ***The Wizard of Earthsea, The Tombs of Atuan, The Farthest Shore, Tehanu, Tales from Earthsea, The Other Wind***, Ursula K. LeGuin. From the first book in the series, where a headstrong young wizard has to confront his own shadow in order to survive, to the last book in the series, which brings the feminine principle in Earthsea back into power and accord with the masculine principle, these books are absolutely awesome. Tonic for the soul. If you've never read LeGuin, start with this series.